Python Programming

A Step-by-Step Guide to Learning the Language

Python Programming

A Step-by-Step Guide to Learning the Language

Dr. C. K. Dhaliwal
Assistant Professor
Chandigarh Business School of Administrations
Mohali, Punjab

***

Poonam Rana
Assistant Professor
Chandigarh Business School of Administrations
Mohali, Punjab

***

Dr. T. P. S. Brar
Professor & Head of Department
Chandigarh Group of Colleges
Mohali, Punjab

CRC Press is an imprint of the
Taylor & Francis Group, an **informa** business

First published 2025
by CRC Press
4 Park Square, Milton Park, Abingdon, Oxon, OX14 4RN

and by CRC Press
2385 NW Executive Center Drive, Suite 320, Boca Raton FL 33431

CRC Press is an imprint of Informa UK Limited

British Library Cataloguing-in-Publication Data
A catalogue record for this book is available from the British Library

ISBN: 9781032646558 (hbk)
ISBN: 9781032669571 (pbk)
ISBN: 9781032691053 (ebk)

DOI: 10.4324/9781032691053

Typeset in Times New Roman
by Manakin Press, Delhi

Organization of the Book

Chapter 1 This is an introductory chapter that provides an overview of Python, covering its history, features, applications, and installation process. It highlights Python's dynamic, high-level, and object-oriented language features and cross-platform compatibility. The chapter emphasizes the use of Python in web development, data science, and machine learning. It also explains Python interactive help and demonstrates how to install and execute Python on different platforms. Additionally, the chapter covers how Python differs from other programming languages.

Chapter 2 This chapter introduces the basics of Python programming language. It covers keywords and identifiers, explaining their differences and how to use them properly. The chapter then moves on to Python statements and demonstrates how to use them to create simple programs. It highlights the importance of documentation and indentation in Python programming. The chapter covers variables and their declaration in Python, including the rules for naming variables. It also covers the different data types in Python, such as numbers, strings, lists, and tuples, along with examples of how to use them.

Chapter 3 This chapter covers Python operators, including arithmetic, relational, logical, bitwise, assignment, and identity operators. It also explains the precedence and associativity of operators, which determine the order in which they are evaluated. The chapter demonstrates how to use expressions, which are combinations of operands and operators, to perform calculations and manipulate data.

Chapter 4 This chapter covers conditional statements in Python, including if, if-else, and if-elif-if statements. It also covers loops in Python, including while, for, and infinite loops, along with examples of how to use them. Additionally, the chapter covers the use of the break, continue, and pass statements in Python loops, which are used to change the flow of control in a program.

Chapter 5 This chapter covers the native data types in Python, including numbers, lists, tuples, sets, dictionaries, and strings. It provides examples and use cases for each data type. The chapter highlights the differences between mutable and immutable data types and how to work with them. Additionally, it covers how to manipulate and operate on data types, including slicing and indexing.

Chapter 6 This chapter covers Python functions, including the types of functions in Python, such as built-in functions, user-defined functions, and anonymous functions. It discusses the advantages of using functions, such as code reusability, modularity, and easier debugging. The chapter also covers the differences between pass by value and pass by reference and demonstrates recursion, which is the ability of a function to call itself.

Chapter 7 This chapter covers Python modules, which are files that contain Python definitions and statements. It demonstrates how to create a module and how to import it into another Python program. Additionally, the chapter covers standard modules, which are built-in modules that come with Python, and Python packages, which are directories containing modules. It highlights how to use and install standard modules and how to create and install Python packages.

Chapter 8 This chapter covers Python exceptions, which are errors that occur during program execution. It explains the different types of built-in exceptions in Python, such as ZeroDivisionError and TypeError. The chapter demonstrates how to handle exceptions using the try-except block and how to raise and catch user-defined exceptions. It also provides examples of exception handling and how to use the else and finally clauses with the try-except block.

Chapter 9 This chapter covers file operations in Python, including how to create, open, read, write, and close files using file methods such as read() and write(). The chapter also covers renaming and deleting files, as well as creating and navigating directories in Python using the os module. It provides examples of how to use file methods and how to handle file exceptions.

Chapter 10 This chapter covers designing classes in Python, which are templates for creating objects that have similar properties and behaviors. It explains how to create objects from a class, how to access object attributes, and how to use built-in class attributes, such as name and doc. The chapter also covers garbage collection in Python, which is the process of freeing up memory that is no longer being used by a program. It provides examples of how to design and use classes in Python.

Chapter 11 This chapter covers inheritance in Python, which is the ability to create a new class from an existing class. It explains the different types of inheritance in Python, including single inheritance, multiple inheritance, and multilevel inheritance. The chapter also covers method overriding in Python, which is the ability to redefine a method in a subclass. Additionally, the chapter discusses special functions in Python, which are predefined methods that are called under certain circumstances, such as init and str. It provides examples of how to use inheritance and special functions in Python.

Chapter 12 This chapter covers operator overloading in Python, which is the ability to redefine the behavior of an operator in a class. It explains how to overload the + and - operators in Python, as well as bitwise and relational operators. The chapter provides examples of how to use operator overloading to customize the behavior of operators in Python.

The Appendix- I is given which provides the list of Python Standard Modules with the description of each.

The bibliography is given at the end for reference of readers.

Authors

Detailed Contents

1

Introduction to Python Language

Highlights

- Introduction and History of Python Language
- Features of Python
- Applications of Python
- Python Interactive Help
- Installing and Executing Python
- How Python Differs from Other Languages

We can see that computers have a wide range of real-world problem-solving abilities. The issues could be as straightforward as multiplying two numbers or as complex as designing and launching a space shuttle. Assuming that a machine can complete all jobs on its own would be wrong. Any problem whose solution is not defined cannot be resolved by a computer. A computer cannot solve any issue whose answer is not known. The computer merely executes the set of instructions that a programmer has provided to it. There may be mistakes and no resolution if the computer cannot comprehend the instructions. As a result, it is the programmer's grave responsibility to come up with a solution by giving the machine the right commands. As a result, it is the programmer's grave responsibility to come up with a solution by giving the machine the right commands.

1.1 Programming Language

A programming language is a formal language used to instruct a computer to perform a specific task or set of tasks. It provides a set of rules and syntax for creating and manipulating code, allowing developers to write programs and applications that can run on a computer.

Programming languages can be classified into different types based on their purpose and structure. Some common types of programming languages include:

1. **Procedural languages:** These languages use a series of steps to solve a problem or accomplish a task. Examples include C, Fortran, and Pascal.
2. **Object-oriented languages:** These languages model the problem as a set of objects that interact with each other to accomplish a task. Examples include Java, Python, and C++.
3. **Functional languages:** These languages focus on the evaluation of expressions and functions, treating them as mathematical equations. Examples include Haskell, Lisp, and ML.
4. **Scripting languages:** These languages are used to automate tasks, such as web development, and are often interpreted rather than compiled. Examples include JavaScript, PHP, and Python.

There are many programming languages in use today, each with its own strengths and weaknesses, and new languages are continually being developed to meet the evolving needs of the technology industry.

Some of the most common programming languages used today include:

1. **Java:** Java is an object-oriented programming language that is widely used for developing enterprise-level applications, mobile applications, and web applications.
2. **Python:** Python is a high-level programming language that is popular for its readability, ease of use, and versatility. It is commonly used for web development, data analysis, and artificial intelligence.
3. **JavaScript:** JavaScript is a scripting language that is used for developing web applications and interactive front-end interfaces.
4. **C#:** C# is an object-oriented programming language that is commonly used for developing Windows desktop applications, video games, and web applications.

5. **C++:** C++ is a high-performance language that is used for developing operating systems, video games, and other resource-intensive applications.
6. **PHP:** PHP is a server-side scripting language that is used for developing dynamic web applications and websites.
7. **Ruby:** Ruby is a high-level scripting language that is known for its simplicity and ease of use. It is commonly used for web development and building web applications.

It is worth noting that the popularity of programming languages can vary depending on factors such as industry trends, the rise of new technologies, and the emergence of new use cases.

1.2 History of Python Language

Python is a high-level, interpreted programming language that was first released in 1991 by its creator, Guido van Rossum. It was designed to be easy to read and write, and to emphasize code readability and simplicity. The origin of the name "Python" comes from a TV show from the 1970s called "Monty Python's Flying Circus". Guido van Rossum is a big fan of the show, and he named the language after it.

Python was initially developed as a hobby project, and its first version was released in February 1991. The language was designed with a clear and concise syntax that allowed developers to write code quickly and efficiently. Python's creators were also focused on making the language easily readable, which has helped to make it popular with beginners and experts alike.

Following are the illustrations of different versions of Python along with the timeline.

In 2000, Python 2.0 was released, which included many new features such as garbage collection, Unicode support, and list comprehensions. This version of the language became the dominant version of Python for many years, and it is still widely used today, despite being officially deprecated as of 2020.

In 2008, Python 3.0 was released, which was a major overhaul of the language that introduced many changes and new features. One of the most significant changes was the removal of backward compatibility with Python 2.x, which made it more difficult for developers to transition to the new version. However, Python 3.0 brought many improvements and new features, including better Unicode support, improved I/O, and more efficient handling of exceptions.

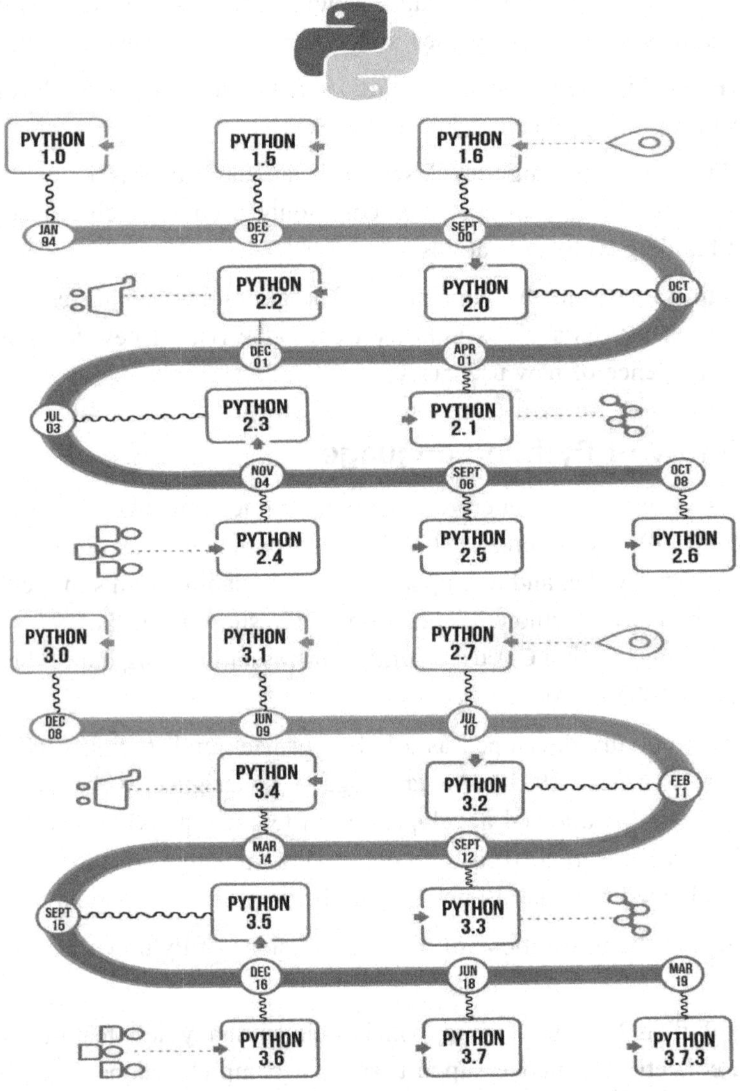

Fig. 1.1: Versions of Python Programming Language.

Today, Python is one of the most popular programming languages in the world, and is used in a wide variety of applications, including web development, data analysis, artificial intelligence, and scientific computing. It is a powerful and flexible language that is well-suited to many different tasks, and it has a large and vibrant community of developers who continue to work on improving the language and developing new libraries and tools.

1.3 Origin of Python Programming Language

Python programming language was created by Guido van Rossum in the late 1980s, while he was working at the Netherlands-based research institute called the National Research Institute for Mathematics and Computer Science (CWI). Guido was tasked with creating a successor to the ABC programming language that was easy to learn and use. He aimed to design a language with an easy-to-understand syntax, which would allow developers to write and maintain code more efficiently.

1.4 Features of Python

Python is a high-level, interpreted programming language that is known for its simplicity, readability, and ease of use. Here are some of the key features of Python:

1. **Simple and easy-to-learn syntax:** Python has a simple and concise syntax, which makes it easy to read and write. Its code is easy to understand, even for beginners, and this simplicity is one of the reasons why Python has become so popular.
2. **Interpreted language:** Python is an interpreted language, which means that you don't need to compile your code before running it. This makes it faster to develop and test code, as you can run it immediately and see the results.
3. **Cross-platform compatibility:** Python code can run on many different platforms, including Windows, Linux, and macOS. This is because Python code is interpreted, and the interpreter is available on all of these platforms.
4. **Large standard library:** Python comes with a large and comprehensive standard library that provides many useful functions and modules for developers. This makes it easy to perform common tasks, such as reading and writing files, working with databases, and performing network operations.
5. **Third-party modules and libraries:** Python has a huge and active community of developers who create and maintain many useful third-party modules and libraries. These libraries provide additional functionality, such as scientific computing, data analysis, web development, and artificial intelligence.

6. **Object-oriented programming support:** Python supports object-oriented programming, which allows developers to write modular, reusable, and maintainable code.
7. **Dynamic typing:** Python is a dynamically-typed language, which means that the type of a variable is determined at runtime, rather than at compile time. This makes it more flexible and allows developers to write code more quickly.
8. **High-level abstractions:** Python provides many high-level abstractions, such as list comprehensions, lambda functions, and decorators, which make it easier to write code that is concise and expressive.

Overall, Python is a powerful and flexible programming language that is well-suited to many different tasks, and its features make it easy to learn and use, even for beginners

1.5 Limitations of Python

While Python is a popular and powerful programming language, it has some limitations that developers should be aware of. Here are some of the main limitations of Python:

1. **Performance:** Python is an interpreted language, which means that it is generally slower than compiled languages like C++ or Java. This can be a limitation when developing applications that require high performance or low latency, such as real-time systems or high-transaction web applications.
2. **Global Interpreter Lock (GIL):** The GIL is a mechanism that ensures that only one thread executes Python bytecode at a time. This can limit the ability of developers to take advantage of multiple processors or cores, which can impact performance.
3. **Weak typing:** While dynamic typing is a key feature of Python, it can also be a limitation in some cases. Without type checking, errors can go undetected until runtime, and the lack of strong typing can make it more difficult to reason about code and catch errors early.

6. **Mobile development:** While Python can be used to develop mobile applications, it is not as well-suited to mobile development as other languages, such as Java or Kotlin. This is because the Android and iOS ecosystems are primarily based on those languages, and they offer more robust support for mobile development.

5. **Memory consumption:** Python is known for its high memory consumption, which can be a limitation when developing applications that need to run on low-memory devices or in constrained environments.
6. **Dependencies and version compatibility:** Python has a large and active community of developers who create and maintain many useful third-party modules and libraries. However, this can lead to version compatibility issues and dependency management challenges.

It's worth noting that many of these limitations can be mitigated by using best practices, such as optimizing code, using appropriate libraries, and following good design principles. Despite these limitations, Python remains a popular and versatile language that is well-suited to many different applications

1.6 Major Applications of Python

Python is a versatile language that can be used for many different applications, from web development to scientific computing. Here are some of the major applications of Python:

1. **Web development:** Python is widely used for web development, both on the server-side and the client-side. Popular web frameworks include Django, Flask, Pyramid, and Bottle.
2. **Data analysis and scientific computing:** Python has become a popular language for data analysis and scientific computing, thanks to libraries such as NumPy, Pandas, SciPy, and Matplotlib. These libraries provide support for numerical operations, data manipulation, statistical analysis, and data visualization.
3. **Machine learning and artificial intelligence:** Python is widely used in the field of machine learning and artificial intelligence, thanks to libraries such as TensorFlow, Keras, PyTorch, and Scikit-learn. These libraries provide support for deep learning, neural networks, natural language processing, and other AI applications.
4. **Desktop applications:** Python can be used to develop desktop applications with graphical user interfaces (GUIs), thanks to libraries such as PyQt, PyGTK, and wxPython.
5. **Game development:** Python is increasingly being used in the field of game development, thanks to libraries such as Pygame and Panda3D.
6. **Automation and scripting:** Python is a popular language for automation and scripting tasks, thanks to its simple syntax and extensive library support.

7. **DevOps**: Python is used in DevOps for automation, testing, and deployment, thanks to libraries such as Fabric and Ansible.
8. **Education:** Python is a popular language for teaching programming, thanks to its simple syntax and ease of use.

Overall, Python is a versatile language that can be used for many different applications, and its popularity and extensive library support make it a valuable tool for developers in many fields.

1.7 Getting Python

Python can be downloaded for free from the official Python website, which provides installers for Windows, macOS, and Linux. Here are the steps to get Python:

1. **Go to the Python website:** Visit the official Python website at https://www.python.org/ and click on the "Downloads" link at the top of the page.
2. **Select your operating system:** Choose your operating system from the list of available options. You can choose between Windows, macOS, and a variety of Linux distributions.
3. **Choose your Python version:** Python is available in two major versions, Python 2 and Python 3. While Python 2 is still in use, it is no longer actively developed and new users are advised to use Python 3. Choose the version of Python that you want to install.
4. **Download the installer:** Once you have chosen your operating system and Python version, download the installer for your system.
5. **Run the installer:** Run the installer on your computer and follow the on-screen instructions to complete the installation process.

After the installation process is complete, you should have access to the Python interpreter and the Python standard library. You can also use an integrated development environment (IDE) such as PyCharm, Spyder, or Jupyter Notebook to write and run Python code.

1.8 Installing Python

Python is a cross-platform programming language, with distributions available for multiple operating systems. To install Python, you can download the binary code for your platform from the official website, and run the installation process. In the event that the binary code is not available for your platform, you can compile the source code manually using a C compiler. The installation process for Python may differ slightly depending on the platform, and specific instructions can be found on the official website for each platform, such as Unix or Linux.

1.8.1 Unix and Linux Installation

Here are the general steps to install Python on Unix or Linux:

1. Open a terminal window.
2. Check if Python is already installed on your system by typing "python" or "python3" into the terminal. If Python is already installed, the version number will be displayed. If Python is not installed, you will see an error message.
3. If Python is not installed, you can install it using your system's package manager. The command may differ depending on your distribution, but some examples are:
   - Ubuntu/Debian: sudo apt-get install python3
   - Red Hat/Fedora: sudo yum install python3
   - Arch Linux: sudo pacman -S python
4. Once the installation is complete, you can verify that Python is installed by typing "python" or "python3" into the terminal.
5. Optionally, you can install a Python IDE or code editor to make it easier to write and run Python code. Popular options include PyCharm, Spyder, Visual Studio Code, and Jupyter Notebook.

1.8.2 Windows Installation

Here are the general steps to install Python on Windows:

1. Go to the official Python website at https://www.python.org/downloads/ and download the latest version of Python 3.x for Windows.
2. Once the installer is downloaded, run the executable file to begin the installation process.
3. In the installation wizard, select "Add Python 3.x to PATH" so that Python can be accessed from the command line and other applications.
4. Choose the "Customize installation" option and make sure that "pip" is selected. This is a package manager that allows you to easily install third-party Python packages.

5. Continue with the installation process by following the on-screen prompts, such as selecting the installation location and accepting the license agreement.
6. Once the installation is complete, you can verify that Python is installed by opening the command prompt and typing "python" followed by the Enter key. This should launch the Python interpreter.
7. Optionally, you can install a Python IDE or code editor to make it easier to write and run Python code. Popular options include PyCharm, Spyder, Visual Studio Code, and Jupyter Notebook.

1.8.3 Macintosh Installation

Here are the general steps to install Python on a Macintosh:

1. Go to the official Python website at https://www.python.org/downloads/ and download the latest version of Python 3.x for Mac.
2. Once the installer is downloaded, open it by double-clicking the .dmg file.
3. Double-click the "Python.mpkg" file to begin the installation process.
4. Follow the on-screen prompts to customize your installation settings, such as the installation directory and any additional components you want to include. The default settings are usually fine for most users.
5. Once the installation is complete, you can verify that Python is installed by opening a terminal window and typing "python3" followed by the Enter key. This should launch the Python interpreter.
6. Optionally, you can install a Python IDE or code editor to make it easier to write and run Python code. Popular options include PyCharm, Spyder, Visual Studio Code, and Jupyter Notebook.

1.9 Setting up Path

Directories can contain various programs and executable files, which means that Windows, Unix/Linux, or MAC operating systems must have a way of finding these files. To locate executable files, the operating system provides a search path that includes directories. This search path is stored in an environment variable, which is a named string that contains information that can be accessed by the command shell and other programs.

1.9.1 Setting up Path at Unix/Linux

To set up the PATH for Python on Unix/Linux, follow these steps:

1. Open a terminal window.
2. Type "nano ~/.bashrc" to open your Bash profile file in the nano text editor.
3. Add the following line to the end of the file, replacing "3.9" with your version of Python:

   export PATH="/usr/local/bin:/usr/bin:/bin:/usr/local/games:/usr/games:/usr/local/python3.9/bin"
4. Save the file by pressing Ctrl + X, then Y, then Enter.
5. Type "source ~/.bashrc" to apply the changes to your current terminal session.
6. You can now run the "python" command from any directory in the terminal.

1.9.2 Setting up the Path at Windows

To set up the PATH for Python on Windows, follow these steps:

1. Right-click on "This PC" or "My Computer" and select "Properties".
2. Click on "Advanced system settings".
3. Click on the "Environment Variables" button at the bottom.
4. Under "System Variables", find the "Path" variable and click "Edit".
5. Click "New" and enter the path to your Python installation directory (e.g. C:\Python39).
6. Click "OK" to close all windows.
7. Open a new command prompt window and type "python" to verify that the PATH has been set up correctly.

1.10 Python Environment Variables

Python uses environment variables to store configuration settings and other system information that can be accessed by your code. Here are some common Python environment variables:

1. **Path:** This variable contains a list of directories where the operating system searches for executable files, including the Python interpreter. When you type "python" in the command prompt, the operating system looks for the "python.exe" file in these directories.
2. **Pythonpath:** This variable contains a list of directories where Python looks for modules and packages. You can add your own directories to this list to make your own modules and packages available to your Python code.
3. **Pythonhome:** This variable points to the root directory of your Python installation. If you move your Python installation to a different directory, you can update this variable to point to the new location.
4. **Pythonstartup:** This variable points to a Python script that is executed every time you start the Python interpreter. You can use this script to define your own Python environment, such as importing modules, defining functions, or setting default values.
5. **Pythonioencoding:** This variable sets the default encoding for input and output streams, such as stdin, stdout, and stderr. By default, Python uses the system's default encoding, but you can change it to a different encoding if needed.

These are just a few examples of Python environment variables. You can access and modify them using the os module in Python.

1.11 Running Python

To run Python code, you first need to install Python on your computer. You can download and install the latest version of Python from the official website: https://www.python.org/downloads/. Once you have installed Python, you can run it in several ways:

1. **Using the Python shell:** The Python shell is an interactive environment that allows you to run Python code line by line. To open the Python shell, simply type "python" in your terminal or command prompt.
2. **Using a text editor:** You can write your Python code in a text editor, save it with a .py file extension, and then run it from the command prompt by typing "python filename.py".
3. **Using an Integrated Development Environment (IDE):** An IDE provides a more advanced environment for writing, debugging, and

running Python code. Some popular IDEs for Python include PyCharm, Visual Studio Code, and Spyder.

Once you have Python installed and set up, you can start writing and running Python code to perform various tasks and solve problems.

1.11.1 Interactive Interpreter

The interactive interpreter in Python is a command-line interface that allows you to enter Python commands and immediately see the results of those commands. It's a great way to experiment with Python and test out code snippets before incorporating them into a larger program.

To launch the Python interpreter, open a terminal or command prompt and type python followed by the Enter key. This will launch the interactive interpreter and display the Python version number and a command prompt (>>>).

You can then enter Python commands at the prompt and see the output immediately. For example, you could type print("Hello, World!") and press Enter, and the interpreter would immediately display the output Hello, World!.

You can exit the interactive interpreter by typing exit() or quit() at the command prompt and pressing Enter. This will return you to the terminal or command prompt.

1.11.2 Script from the Command-Line

You can run a Python script from the command-line by typing python followed by the name of the script file. Here's an example:

Suppose you have a script called hello.py that contains the following code:

```
print("Hello, World!")
```

To run this script, open a terminal or command prompt and navigate to the directory where hello.py is saved. Then, type the following command and press Enter:

```
python hello.py
```

This will execute the script, and you should see the output Hello, World! in the terminal or command prompt.

You can also pass command-line arguments to a Python script by including them after the script name. For example, if you have a script called add.py that takes two numbers as arguments and adds them together, you could run it with the following command:

```
python add.py 2 3
```

This would execute the script with the arguments 2 and 3, and the output would be 5.

Note that in order to run a Python script from the command-line, you must have Python installed on your computer and the Python executable must be in your system's PATH variable.

1.11.3 Integrated Development Environment

An Integrated Development Environment (IDE) is a software application that provides a comprehensive environment for writing, testing, and debugging software code. Python has many popular IDEs that provide features like syntax highlighting, code completion, debugging tools, and more. Some popular Python IDEs include:

1. **PyCharm:** PyCharm is a powerful and full-featured IDE for Python. It includes advanced code completion, debugging tools, and support for web development frameworks like Django and Flask.
2. **Visual Studio Code:** Visual Studio Code is a lightweight and versatile IDE that supports a wide range of programming languages, including Python. It includes features like syntax highlighting, code completion, and debugging tools.
3. **Spyder:** Spyder is an IDE designed specifically for scientific computing and data analysis in Python. It includes features like variable explorer, data viewer, and plotting tools.
4. **IDLE:** IDLE is a simple and lightweight IDE that comes bundled with Python. It includes basic features like syntax highlighting and debugging tools.

There are many other IDEs available for Python, and the best one for you will depend on your specific needs and preferences. You can download and install most Python IDEs for free, and they are available for all major operating systems.

1.12 First Python Program

Python is a popular high-level programming language that is known for its simplicity, readability, and versatility. It is widely used for a variety of purposes, including web development, data analysis, machine learning, and more.

One of the reasons that Python is so popular is its syntax, which is designed to be easy to read and write. For example, instead of using curly braces and semicolons to denote code blocks and statements, Python uses whitespace and indentation. Here is an example of a simple Python program that prints a message to the console:

```
print("Hello, World!")
```

This program simply uses the print() function to display the message "Hello, World!" on the console. You can save this code to a file with a .py extension, such as hello.py, and then execute it from the command line by typing python hello.py.

1.12.1 Interactive Mode Programming

In Python, you can also run programs in interactive mode, which allows you to enter code directly into the Python interpreter and immediately see the output. This is a great way to experiment with Python and test out code snippets before incorporating them into a larger program.

To launch the interactive interpreter in Python, open a terminal or command prompt and type python followed by the Enter key. This will launch the interpreter and display the Python version number and a command prompt (>>>).

You can then enter Python commands at the prompt and see the output immediately. For example, you could type print("Hello, World!") and press Enter, and the interpreter would immediately display the output Hello, World!.

In interactive mode, you can also define variables, create functions, and import modules, just as you would in a regular Python program. For example, you could define a variable like this:

```
x = 5
```

And then use it in a calculation like this:

```
y = x * 2
print(y)
```

This would define a variable x with the value 5, and then define a variable y with the value 10 (which is the result of multiplying x by 2). Finally, it would print the value of y to the console.

You can exit the interactive interpreter by typing exit() or quit() at the command prompt and pressing Enter. This will return you to the terminal or command prompt.

1.12.2 The Script Mode Programming

In addition to running Python code in interactive mode, you can also write code in a file and run it as a script. This is a common way to write larger Python programs that can be executed from the command line or scheduled to run automatically.

To create a Python script, simply create a new file with a .py extension and write your code in it using a text editor or integrated development environment (IDE). For example, you could create a file called hello.py and write the following code:

```
print("Hello, World!")
```

To run this script, you can execute it from the command line by typing python hello.py and pressing Enter. This will run the script and print the message "Hello, World!" to the console.

In a Python script, you can include any valid Python code, including importing modules, defining functions, and using control structures like loops and conditionals. For example, you could write a more complex script that asks the user for their name and then greets them:

```
name = input("What is your name? ")
print("Hello, " + name + "!")
```

This script would prompt the user to enter their name using the input() function, and then use string concatenation to print a personalized greeting.

Overall, writing Python scripts is a powerful way to build complex programs that can be used in a variety of contexts. With a little practice, you can use Python to automate repetitive tasks, process data, and build sophisticated applications.

1.13 Python's Interactive Help

Python comes with a built-in help utility, which is one of the major features and support of Python language. The prerequisite of using the built-in help of Python, you must have a little knowledge of programming. For a new programmer, it could be a bit off-putting. Once a programmer becomes familiar with programming terminology then he can make great use of the built-in help provided by Python. Python programming help can be obtained in the following ways:

- Interactive mode help
- Getting help online through a web browser

1.13.1 Python Help Through a Web Browser

Python has an extensive standard library, as well as a large and active community of developers who have created many third-party modules and libraries. As a result, there are many resources available for getting help with Python online.

One popular resource is the Python documentation, which is available online in a web browser at the official Python website (https://www.python.org/). The documentation includes a detailed language reference, as well as tutorials and guides for getting started with Python, building web applications, working with data, and more.

In addition to the official Python documentation, there are many online forums and communities where you can ask questions and get help with Python. For example, the Python subreddit (https://www.reddit.com/r/Python/) is a popular forum where Python users can ask questions, share code snippets, and get advice from other developers.

There are also many third-party websites and services that offer Python tutorials, courses, and other learning resources. For example, Codecademy (https://www.codecademy.com/learn/learn-python) offers a comprehensive Python course for beginners, while Udemy (https://www.udemy.com/topic/python/) has a wide range of Python courses for learners of all levels.

Overall, there are many resources available for getting help with Python online, and the best approach will depend on your specific needs and learning style. Whether you're a beginner or an experienced developer, there are many ways to learn and grow your skills with Python.

1.14 Python Differences From Other Languages

While the Python language shares some similarities with C, C++, and Java, there are also distinct differences that set it apart from these languages.

1.14.1 Difference Between C and Python

C and Python are both popular programming languages, but they differ in several ways. Here are some of the main differences between C and Python:

1. **Syntax:** C uses a more complex syntax than Python. C requires more code to accomplish the same tasks as Python, and it also has stricter rules for formatting and organization.
2. **Compiled vs. Interpreted:** C is a compiled language, meaning that the code is translated into machine code by a compiler before it can be executed. Python, on the other hand, is an interpreted language, meaning that the code is executed directly by an interpreter.
3. **Typing:** C is a statically typed language, meaning that the type of each variable is declared explicitly in the code. Python, on the other hand, is a dynamically typed language, meaning that the type of each variable is determined at runtime.
4. **Memory Management:** C requires manual memory management, meaning that the programmer must explicitly allocate and deallocate memory for variables and data structures. Python, on the other hand, has automatic memory management, meaning that the interpreter takes care of memory allocation and deallocation.
5. **Application:** C is often used for low-level systems programming, such as operating systems, device drivers, and embedded systems, as well as for high-performance computing and graphics programming. Python is often used for web development, data analysis, scientific computing, and automation.
6. **Object-Oriented Programming:** While C supports object-oriented programming (OOP), it is not a pure OOP language like Python. Python is designed to support OOP concepts such as encapsulation, inheritance, and polymorphism, making it easier to write and organize code for larger projects.
7. **Platform Independence:** Python is more platform-independent than C, meaning that Python code can run on a variety of operating systems and hardware without modification. C code, on the other hand, may need to be recompiled for different platforms or architectures.
8. **Libraries and Packages:** Python has a vast library of built-in modules and third-party packages that make it easy to perform a wide range of tasks, from web scraping to machine learning. C has a smaller standard

library and fewer third-party packages, making it more difficult to find pre-built solutions for common programming problems.

9. **Debugging:** Debugging C code can be more challenging than debugging Python code, due to C's lower-level nature and manual memory management. Python has built-in debugging tools and a more forgiving syntax, making it easier to locate and fix errors in code.
10. **Learning Curve:** Python is generally considered to be easier to learn and use than C, due to its simpler syntax, automatic memory management, and built-in data structures. C requires a deeper understanding of computer architecture and low-level programming concepts, making it more difficult to learn and master.

These are just a few of the many differences between C and Python. While they share some similarities, they are distinct languages with their own strengths and weaknesses, and the choice of language will depend on the specific needs of the project and the preferences of the programmer.

1.14.2 Difference Between C++ and Python

C++ and Python are both popular programming languages, but they differ in several ways. Here are some of the main differences between C++ and Python:

1. **Syntax:** C++ uses a more complex syntax than Python. C++ requires more code to accomplish the same tasks as Python, and it also has stricter rules for formatting and organization.
2. **Compiled vs. Interpreted:** C++ is a compiled language, meaning that the code is translated into machine code by a compiler before it can be executed. Python, on the other hand, is an interpreted language, meaning that the code is executed directly by an interpreter.
3. **Typing:** C++ is a statically typed language, meaning that the type of each variable is declared explicitly in the code. Python, on the other hand, is a dynamically typed language, meaning that the type of each variable is determined at runtime.
4. **Memory Management:** C++ requires manual memory management, meaning that the programmer must explicitly allocate and deallocate memory for variables and data structures. Python, on the other hand, has automatic memory management, meaning that the interpreter takes care of memory allocation and deallocation.

5. **Object-Oriented Programming:** Both C++ and Python support object-oriented programming (OOP), but C++ is often considered a "pure" OOP language, meaning that all code is organized into objects and classes. Python, on the other hand, allows for more procedural and functional programming styles as well.
6. **Application:** C++ is often used for systems programming, such as operating systems and device drivers, as well as for high-performance computing, gaming, and graphics programming. Python is often used for web development, data analysis, scientific computing, and automation.
7. **Libraries and Packages:** Python has a vast library of built-in modules and third-party packages that make it easy to perform a wide range of tasks, from web scraping to machine learning. C++ has a smaller standard library and fewer third-party packages, making it more difficult to find pre-built solutions for common programming problems.
8. **Speed:** C++ is generally faster than Python because it is a compiled language, meaning that the code is translated into machine code before it is executed. Python, on the other hand, is an interpreted language, meaning that the code is executed directly by an interpreter, which can be slower. However, Python has some libraries that are implemented in C or C++ that can boost its performance.
9. **Learning Curve:** C++ is generally considered more difficult to learn and use than Python. C++ has a steep learning curve because it is a more complex language with a larger number of features and more stringent syntax rules. Python, on the other hand, has a simpler syntax and a smaller set of features, making it easier to learn and use.
10. **Type Safety:** C++ is a type-safe language, meaning that the compiler checks for type errors at compile time. Python is not type-safe, meaning that type errors can occur at runtime.
11. **Multithreading:** C++ has built-in support for multithreading, allowing programs to execute multiple threads of code concurrently. Python also supports multithreading, but it has a global interpreter lock (GIL) that can limit the performance gains of multithreading in some cases.
12. **Portability:** Python is more portable than C++ because it is a high-level language that can be interpreted on any platform. C++ code must be compiled on the specific platform it will run on, which can make it less portable.

13. **Memory Safety:** C++ is a language that provides the programmer with the ability to manually manage memory. While this gives the programmer more control over how memory is used, it also means that the program can be susceptible to memory-related bugs, such as buffer overflows and memory leaks. Python has built-in garbage collection, meaning that it automatically manages memory, which makes it less susceptible to memory-related bugs.

These are just a few of the many differences between C++ and Python. While both languages are widely used and powerful, they have different strengths and weaknesses, and the choice of language will depend on the specific needs of the project and the preferences of the programmer.

1.14.3 Difference between Java and Python

Java and Python are both popular programming languages, but they differ in several ways. Here are some of the main differences between Java and Python:

1. **Syntax:** Java has a more complex syntax than Python. Java requires more code to accomplish the same tasks as Python, and it also has stricter rules for formatting and organization
2. **Compiled vs. Interpreted:** Java is a compiled language, meaning that the code is translated into bytecode by a compiler before it can be executed. Python, on the other hand, is an interpreted language, meaning that the code is executed directly by an interpreter.
3. **Typing:** Java is a statically typed language, meaning that the type of each variable is declared explicitly in the code. Python, on the other hand, is a dynamically typed language, meaning that the type of each variable is determined at runtime.
4. **Memory Management:** Java has automatic memory management, meaning that the JVM (Java Virtual Machine) takes care of memory allocation and deallocation. Python also has automatic memory management, meaning that the interpreter takes care of memory allocation and deallocation.
5. **Object-Oriented Programming:** Both Java and Python support object-oriented programming (OOP), and they have similar concepts such as inheritance, polymorphism, and encapsulation. However, Java is often considered a “pure” OOP language, meaning that all code is organized

into objects and classes. Python, on the other hand, allows for more procedural and functional programming styles as well.

6. **Application:** Java is often used for web development, desktop application development, and mobile app development. Python is often used for web development, scientific computing, data analysis, machine learning, and automation.
7. **Performance:** Java is generally faster than Python because it is a compiled language, and the JVM can optimize the bytecode for performance. Python, on the other hand, is an interpreted language, meaning that the code is executed directly by an interpreter, which can be slower. However, Python has some libraries that are implemented in C or C++ that can boost its performance.
8. **Garbage Collection:** Java has a more advanced garbage collector than Python, meaning that it can handle memory more efficiently.
9. **Learning Curve:** Java is generally considered more difficult to learn and use than Python. Java has a steep learning curve because it is a more complex language with a larger number of features and more stringent syntax rules. Python, on the other hand, has a simpler syntax and a smaller set of features, making it easier to learn and use.

These are just a few of the many differences between Java and Python. While both languages are widely used and powerful, they have different strengths and weaknesses, and the choice of language will depend on the specific needs of the project and the preferences of the programmer.

1.15 Summary

In this chapter, we have learned about the programming language and its needs. Then we gave a brief look at the origin and history of the Python language along with its features and limitations. We have explored in detail how Python language differs from other existing and prominent programming languages such as C,C++, and Java. The setup and installation of Python language along with a simple first program are also discussed in detail.

Review Questions

1. What is Python and what makes it a popular programming language?
2. How does Python differ from other programming languages?

3. What is the history of the Python programming language and who developed it?
4. What are the steps to install Python on different operating systems?
5. What are the benefits of using Python for software development?
6. What are the key features of Python, and how do they contribute to its popularity?
7. How does the Python community support and contribute to the language's development?
8. What are some popular applications built using Python?
9. How does Python compare with other programming languages like Java, C++, and Ruby?
10. What are the most important considerations when choosing a programming language, and how does Python measure up?
11. What is Python and how is it used?
12. Python is a high-level programming language used for a variety of applications, including web development, data analysis, artificial intelligence, and more.
13. Python is a type of reptile found in tropical regions around the world.
14. What are some key features of the Python programming language?
    a. Python has a simple and easy-to-learn syntax.
    b. Python is an interpreted language, meaning that code is executed directly by an interpreter without the need for compilation.

2

Python Data Types and Input Output

Highlights

- Keywords and identifiers
- Python statements
- Documentation and indentation
- Python Variables
- Python data types
- Input and output
- Import

Python has several built-in data types including strings, integers, and lists. These data types can be used to store and manipulate different kinds of information in a program. In addition to these basic data types, Python also has advanced data types such as dictionaries and sets.

Python also has a built-in module for input/output operations, which allows a program to read from and write to external sources, such as files and streams. The module, called io, provides several functions to perform these operations, such as open(), read(), and write().

2.1 Keywords

In Python, a keyword is a word that has a special meaning in the Python language. Keywords are used to define the syntax and structure of the

Python language, and they cannot be used as identifiers (i.e., variable names, function names, etc.) in Python code.

Keyword	Description
and	Logical operator returns True if both operands are True, otherwise, it returns False.
as	Used to create an alias for a module or variable when importing or renaming.
assert	Used to check if a given condition is True, and raises an exception if it is False.
async	Used to define an asynchronous function or context manager.
await	Used inside an async function to wait for an asynchronous operation to complete.
break	Used to exit a loop early, before the loop condition is met.
class	Used to define a new class.
continue	Used to skip the current iteration of a loop and continue with the next iteration.
def	Used to define a new function.
del	Used to delete an object or an item from a collection.
elif	Short for "else if", used in a conditional statement to check for additional conditions.
else	Used in a conditional statement as a catch-all option if no other conditions are met.
except	Used to handle exceptions that are raised in a try block.
False	Boolean value that represents the absence of truth.
finally	Used in a try-except block to specify a block of code that will always be executed, regardless of whether an exception was raised or not.
for	Used to iterate over a sequence of items, such as a list or a tuple.
from	Used in an import statement to import specific items from a module.
global	Used to indicate that a variable is a global variable, accessible from anywhere in the code.
if	Used to start a conditional statement.
import	Used to import a module or a specific item from a module.

Keyword	Description
in	Used to check if an item is in a sequence, such as a list or a tuple.
is	Used to check if two variables refer to the same object.
lambda	Used to create small anonymous functions.
None	Special value that represents the absence of a value or a null value.
nonlocal	Used to indicate that a variable is nonlocal to the current function, meaning it is defined in an outer function.
not	Logical operator that negates a boolean value.
or	Logical operator that returns True if at least one of the operands is True, otherwise it returns False.
pass	Used as a placeholder for a block of code that does nothing.
raise	Used to raise an exception.
return	Used to exit a function and return a value to the calling code.
True	Boolean value that represents the presence of truth.
try	Used to specify a block of code that might raise an exception.
while	Used to start a loop that will continue to execute as long as the loop condition is True.
with	Used to create a context manager, which is used to automatically set up and tear down resources.
yield	Used in a function

2.2 Identifiers

In Python, an identifier is a name used to identify a variable, function, class, module, or other objects. There are a few rules and conventions for naming identifiers in Python:

- Identifiers must start with a letter or an underscore (_).
- Identifiers cannot start with a number.
- Identifiers can only contain letters, numbers, and underscores.
- Identifiers are case-sensitive, so myVariable and myvariable are considered to be different identifiers.
- Python reserves a set of keywords that cannot be used as identifiers. Examples include if, else, for, class, etc.

- Identifiers should be descriptive and meaningful, using camelCase or snake_case, depending on the project's style guide.

Examples of valid identifiers in Python:

- myVariable
- _privateVariable
- counter
- calculate_average
- MyClass

Examples of invalid identifiers in Python:

- 1stVariable (starts with a number)
- my-variable (contains a hyphen)
- if (reserved keyword)
- True (reserved keyword)
- class (reserved keyword)

2.3 Python Statements

In Python, a statement is a single line of code that performs a specific action or instruction. There are several types of statements in Python, including:

- **Expressions:** These are statements that evaluate to a value, such as mathematical operations or function calls. Examples include "2 + 2" or "print('Hello, world!')".
- **Assignment statements:** These are statements that assign a value to a variable. Examples include "x = 2" or "name = 'John'".
- **Control flow statements:** These are statements that control the flow of execution of a program, such as conditional statements (if/else) and loops (for/while).
- **Function and class definitions:** These are statements that define a function or class, respectively. Examples include "def my_function():" and "class MyClass:".
- **Import statements:** These statements are used to import modules or packages in python. Examples include "import os" or "from math import sqrt"

- **Pass statements**: A pass statement is a null operation. Nothing happens when it executes. It is useful as a placeholder when a statement is required syntactically, but no code needs to be executed.

2.4 Indentation

Indentation is used in Python to indicate blocks of code. The standard indentation is four spaces, and most Python code follows this convention. For example

Code 2.1 Illustration of indentation in Python

```
def foo():
    # This line is indented by four spaces
    x = 5
    if x > 0:
        # This line is also indented by four spaces
        print("x is positive")
    # This line is not indented, so it's not part of the if block
```

It is important to be consistent with your indentation, as the meaning of the code can change based on the indentation level. For example

Code 2.2 Illustration of indentation in Python

```
x = 5
if x > 0:
    print("x is positive")
print("This line is not indented, so it's not part of the if block")
```

This code will print both messages because the second print statement is not indented, so it is not part of the if block.

Code 2.3 Illustration of indentation in Python

```
x = 5
if x > 0:
    print("x is positive")
    print("This line is indented, so it is part of the if block")
print("This line is not indented, so it's not part of the if block")
```

This code will only print the first message, because the second print statement is indented, so it is part of the if block.

2.5 Python Documentation

In Python, documentation is typically included in the form of comments in the source code. These comments start with a # symbol, and everything following the # on that line is considered a comment. For example:

Code 2.4 Illustration of documentation in Python using #

```
# This is a comment
x = 5  # This is also a comment
```

2.5.1 Single Line Comment

In Python, a single line comment is created by placing the "#" symbol at the beginning of the line, followed by the text of the comment. For example:

Code 2.5 Illustration of single line documentation in Python

```
# This is a single line comment in Python
x = 10  # This is also a single line comment
```

The text following the "#" symbol is ignored by the Python interpreter and is only there for the benefit of the person reading the code. Single line comments are often used to add brief explanations or clarifications to the code.

Code 2.6 Illustration of single line documentation in Python

```
# Calculate the area of a rectangle
width = 3
height = 12
area = width * height
```

In this example, the single line comments provide some context for the code that follows, explaining what the variables are used for and what the final line of code is doing.

2.5.2 Multi Line Comments

In Python, multi-line comments can be created using triple quotes, either single quotes (‘’’) or double quotes (“”””). The comments can span multiple lines and are commonly used for longer explanations and docstrings. Here is an example:

Code 2.7 Illustration of double quotes in Python

```
"""
This is a multiline
comment. It can span
multiple lines.
"""
```

You can also use triple single quotes to create a multiline comment:

Code 2.8 Illustration of single quotes in Python

```
'''
This is also a
multiline comment. It
can also span multiple
lines.
'''
```

Both triple quotes (single or double) can be used to create a multiline comment in Python. The advantage of using triple quotes is that you can create a multiline comment even if it contains multiple lines of the same type of quote character.

2.6 Docstrings

In Python, a docstring is a string literal that appears as the first statement in a module, function, class, or method definition. It is used to provide documentation for the code, and can be accessed using the built-in help() function or the __doc__ attribute. Docstrings are enclosed in triple quotes (either single or double) and are typically written in plain text, but can also include markdown formatting.

It is a good practice to include a docstring in any function or class you write, as it makes your code more readable and user-friendly.

Here is an example of a simple Python function with a docstring:

Code 2.9 Illustration of docstring in Python

```
def add(a, b):
    """
    This function takes two numbers as input and returns their sum.

    Parameters:
    a (int): The first number
    b (int): The second number

    Returns:
    int: The sum of a and b
    """
    return a + b
```

In this example, the function add takes two numbers as input, adds them together, and returns the result. The docstring provides a brief description of what the function does, and explains the parameters and return value.

To access the docstring of this function, you can use the help() function like this:

```
help(add)
```

You can also access the docstring programmatically using the __doc__ attribute:

```
print(add.__doc__)
```

This will output the same string as the docstring.

By providing clear and concise documentation, it's easy for other developers to understand how the function works, what the parameters are and what to expect when calling the function. This can save a lot of time and effort when working on large projects with multiple contributors.

2.7 Variables

A Python variable is a reserved memory location to store values. In other words, a variable in a python program gives data to the computer for processing. Every value in Python has a datatype. Different data types in Python are Numbers, List, Tuple, Strings, Dictionary, etc. Variables can be declared by any name or even alphabets like a, aa, abc, etc.

2.7.1 Variable Assignment

Think of a variable as a name attached to a particular object. In Python, variables need not be declared or defined in advance, as is the case in many other programming languages. To create a variable, you just assign it a value and then start using it. The assignment is done with a single equals sign (=):

```
n = 300
```

This is read or interpreted as "n is assigned the value 300." Once this is done, n can be used in a statement or expression, and its value will be substituted:

```
print(n)
300
```

Just as a literal value can be displayed directly from the interpreter prompt in a REPL session without the need for print(), so can a variable:

```
n
300
```

Later, if you change the value of n and use it again, the new value will be substituted instead:

```
n = 1000
 print(n)
1000
```

Python also allows chained assignment, which makes it possible to assign the same value to several variables simultaneously:

Code 2.10 Illustration of variable in Python

```
a = b = c = 300
print(a, b, c)
300 300 300
```

2.7.2 Variable Types in Python

In many programming languages, variables are statically typed. That means a variable is initially declared to have a specific data type, and any value assigned to it during its lifetime must always have that type. Variables in Python are not subject to this restriction. In Python, a variable may be assigned a value of one type and then later re-assigned a value of a different type:

Code 2.11 Illustration of variable in Python

```
var = 21.09
print(var)
21.09
```

Let's see another example:

Code 2.12 Illustration of variable in Python

```
>>> var = "Welcome to Python"
>>> print(var)
Welcome to Python
```

2.8 Multiple Assignment

Multiple assignment allows you to assign multiple variables at the same time in one line of code. This feature often seems simple after you've learned about it, but it can be tricky to recall multiple assignment when you need it most. In this we'll see what multiple assignment is, we'll take a look at common uses of multiple assignment, and then we'll look at a few uses for multiple assignment that are often overlooked.

Python's multiple assignment looks like this:

```
>>> x, y = 10, 20
```

Here we're setting x to 10 and y to 20.

What's happening at a lower level is that we're creating a tuple of 10, 20 and then looping over that tuple and taking each of the two items we get from looping and assigning them to x and y in order.

This syntax might make that a bit more clear:

```
>>> (x, y) = (10, 20)
```

Parenthesis are optional around tuples in Python and they're also optional in multiple assignment (which uses a tuple-like syntax). All of these are equivalent:

Code 2.13 Illustration of variable in Python

```
>>> x, y = 10, 20
>>> x, y = (10, 20)
>>> (x, y) = 10, 20
>>> (x, y) = (10, 20)
```

Multiple assignments are often called "tuple unpacking" because it's frequently used with tuples. But we can use multiple assignments with any iterable, not just tuples. Here we're using it with a list:

Code 2.13 Illustration of variable in Python

```
>>> x, y = [10, 20]
>>> x
10
>>> y
20
```

And with a string:

Code 2.13 Illustration of a variable with a string in Python

```
>>> x, y = 'hi'
>>> x
'h'
>>> y
'i'
```

Here's another example to demonstrate that multiple assignments works with any number of items and that it works with variables as well as objects we've just created:

Code 2.14 Illustration of a variable in Python

```
>>> point = 10, 20, 30
>>> x, y, z = point
>>> print(x, y, z)
10 20 30
>>> (x, y, z) = (z, y, x)
>>> print(x, y, z)
30 20 10
```

2.9 Python Data Types

Data types are the classification or categorization of data items. It represents the kind of value that tells what operations can be performed on a particular data. Since everything is an object in Python programming, data types are actually classes and variables are instances (objects) of these classes.

Following are the standard or built-in data types of Python:

- Numeric
- Sequence Type
- Boolean
- Set
- Dictionary

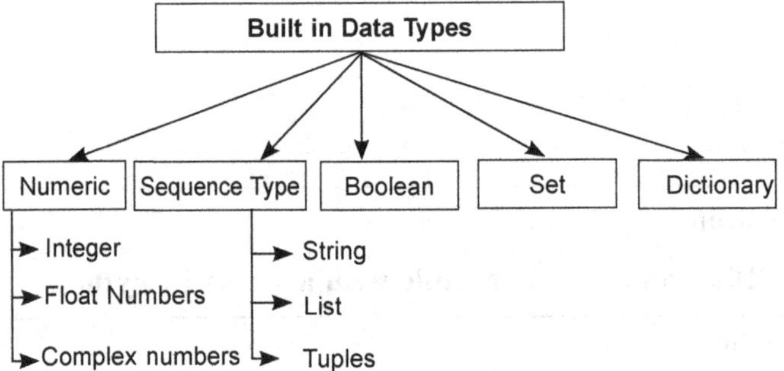

In Python, there are several built-in data types that you can use to store values in your program. These data types include

1. **Integers:** These are whole numbers, both positive and negative. For example 42, -7, 0.
2. **Floating-point numbers:** These are numbers with a decimal point, such as 3.14 or -0.01.
3. **Complex Numbers:** These are the numbers that has both a real and an imaginary component. For example 3+6j.
4. **Strings:** These are sequences of characters, represented using quotes. You can use single quotes (') or double quotes (") to represent strings. For example: 'hello', "world", '42'.
5. **Booleans**: These represent truth values and can be either True or False.
6. **Lists:** These are ordered collections of other values. You can define a list by enclosing a comma-separated sequence of values in square brackets ([]). For example: [1, 2, 3], ['a', 'b', 'c'], [True, False].

7. **Tuples:** These are like lists, but they are immutable (i.e., you cannot modify them). You can define a tuple by enclosing a comma-separated sequence of values in parentheses (()). For example: (1, 2, 3), ('a', 'b', 'c'), (True, False).
8. **Sets:** These are unordered collections of unique values. You can define a set by enclosing a comma-separated sequence of values in curly braces ({}). For example: {1, 2, 3}, {'a', 'b', 'c'}, {True, False}.
9. **Dictionaries:** These are unordered collections of key-value pairs. You can define a dictionary by enclosing a comma-separated sequence of key-value pairs in curly braces ({}). The key and value are separated by a colon (:). For example: {'a': 1, 'b': 2, 'c': 3}, {'a': 'A', 'b': 'B', 'c': 'C'}, {True: 'Yes', False: 'No'}.

2.9.1 Numeric Datatype

In Python, the Number datatype includes integers (int), floating-point numbers (float), and complex numbers (complex).

1. **Integers:** Integers are whole numbers without a decimal point, such as 1, 2, and 100.
2. **Floating-point numbers** have a decimal point, such as 3.14 and 2.71828.
3. **Complex numbers** have a real and imaginary component, such as 3 + 4j. Python also has support for arbitrary precision integers using the 'decimal' module and for large integers using the 'bigint' module.

2.9.1.1 Integers

In Python, an integer is a whole number that can be positive, negative, or zero. It has no fractional part and is represented by a series of digits. For example, the integers 123, -456, and 0 are all integers. To create an integer in Python, you can simply assign a whole number to a variable. For example:

Code 2.15 Illustration of integer number data types

```
x = 123
y = -456
z = 0
```

You can also use the int() function to convert a string or a floating-point number to an integer. For example

Code 2.16 Illustration of floating-point number data types

```
x = int("123")
y = int(-456.7)
z = int(7.9)
```

In the second example, the float -456.7 is converted to the integer -456, and in the third example, the float 7.9 is converted to the integer 7. You can perform various arithmetic operations on integers, such as addition, subtraction, multiplication, and division. For example

Code 2.17 Illustration of arithmetic operations

```
x = 2 + 3
y = 4 - 1
z = 2 * 3
w = 8 / 3
```

In Python, the / operator always performs floating-point division, even if both operands are integers. To perform integer division, you can use the // operator. For example:

```
x = 8 // 3
```

This will give the result 2, as the remainder is discarded in integer division.

You can also use the % operator to find the remainder of an integer division. For example:

```
x = 8 % 3
```

This will give the result 2, as the remainder of 8 divided by 3 is 2.

2.9.1.2 Floating-point Numbers

In Python, a floating-point number is a numerical value with a decimal point. For example, 3.14, 4.0, and 0.01 are all floating-point numbers. In Python, you can use the "float" data type to represent a floating-point number. Here are some examples of how to create and use floating-point numbers in Python:

Code 2.18 Illustration of floating-point number data types

```
x = 3.14  # assign the value 3.14 to x
y = 4.0   # assign the value 4.0 to y
z = 0.01  # assign the value 0.01 to z
# You can perform arithmetic with floating-point numbers just like with integers:
a = x + y  # a is now 7.14
b = y / z  # b is now 400.0
```

It's important to note that floating-point arithmetic is not always completely precise. For example, the result of the expression "0.1 + 0.2" might not be exactly 0.3 due to the way that computers represent and store decimal values. However, this usually doesn't cause any significant problems in practice.

2.9.1.3 Complex Numbers

In Python, a complex number is a number that has both a real and an imaginary component. The real component is represented by a floating-point number, and the imaginary component is represented by the letter "j" or "J". You can create a complex number by adding a real and an imaginary component together, using the "+" operator. For example:

```
x = 3 + 4j
```

You can also create a complex number using the built-in complex() function. For example:

```
x = complex(3, 4)
```

You can access the real and imaginary components of a complex number using the real and imag attributes, respectively. For example:

Code 2.19 Illustration of complex number data types

```
x = 3 + 4j
print(x.real) # Output: 3.0
print(x.imag) # Output: 4.0
```

You can also perform mathematical operations with complex numbers, such as addition, subtraction, multiplication, and division. For example:

Code 2.20 Illustration of mathematical operations with complex numbers

```
x = 3 + 4j
y = 2 + 3j
print(x + y) # Output: (5+7j)
print(x - y) # Output: (1+1j)
print(x * y) # Output: (-6+17j)
print(x / y) # Output: (1.6+0.4j)
```

2.9.2 Strings

In Python, a string is a sequence of characters enclosed in quotation marks. You can use either single quotes or double quotes to create a string. For example:

```
string1 = 'Hello, world!'
string2 = "Hello, world!"
```

Both of these expressions create a string with the value "Hello, world!".

You can use the "+" operator to concatenate (join) two strings together. For example:

Code 2.21 Illustration of Strings in Python

```
greeting = "Hello"
name = "Alice"
message = greeting + ", " + name + "!"
print(message) # prints "Hello, Alice!"
repeat = "*" * 10
print(repeat) # prints "**********"
```

There are many other operations and methods available for working with strings in Python. You can learn more about strings in the Python documentation.

2.9.2.1 Indexing of a String:

In Python, strings can be indexed (i.e., reference a specific character in the string) using square brackets [] and the index of the desired character. The indexing starts from 0, so the first character has an index of 0, the second character has an index of 1, and so on.

Here is an example:

Code 2.22 Illustration of indexing in Python

```
string = "Hello, World!"
print(string[0]) # Output: 'H'
print(string[7]) # Output: 'W'
```

2.9.2.2 Negative Indexing:

Python also allows negative indexing of a string that starts counting from the right side of the string. The rightmost character has an index of -1, the second character from the right has an index of -2, and so on.

0	1	2	3	4	5	6	7	8	9
H	E	L	L	O	W	O	R	L	D
-11	-10	-9	-8	-7	-6	-5	-4	-3	-2

Code 2.23 Illustration of negative indexing in Python

```
string = "HelloWorld"
print(string[-1]) # Output: 'd'
print(string[-3]) # Output: 'r'
```

2.9.2.3 Slicing

Negative indexing can use to extract a range of characters from a string or to extract a substring from a string by specifying the start and end index separated by a colon : , known as slicing. The syntax for slicing is string[start:stop:step], where start is the index of the first character to include stop is the index of the first character to exclude and step is the number of indices between characters

Code 2.24 Illustration of slicing operator in Python

```
string = "Hello, World!"
print(string[7:12]) # Output: 'World'
print(string[:5])   # Output: 'Hello'
print(string[7:])   # Output: 'World!'
```

You can also use negative indexing and positive indexing together in the slicing.

Code 2.25 Illustration of negative and positive indexing in Python

```
string = "Hello, World!"
print(string[0:-1]) # Output: 'Hello, World'
print(string[-12:5]) # Output: 'Hello'
```

2.9.3 Booleans

In Python, a boolean is a data type that represents one of two values: True or False. Booleans are often used to represent the truth value of an expression or to represent the state of a toggle. Here are a few examples of boolean expressions in Python:

Code 2.26 Illustration of Booleans in Python

```
>>> 2 < 3
True
>>> 2 > 3
False
>>> 3 == 3
True
>>> 'hello' == 'goodbye'
False
>>> True and False
False
>>> True or False
True
```

You can also use boolean values in control statements such as if and while to execute code conditionally. For example:

Code 2.26 Illustration of Booleans values in control statements

```
>>> x = 10
>>> if x > 5:
>>>     print('x is greater than 5')
x is greater than 5
```

2.9.4 Lists

In Python, a list is an ordered collection of objects. You can create a list by enclosing a comma-separated sequence of objects in square brackets ([]). For example:

Code 2.27 Illustration of List in Python

```
>>> a = [1, 2, 3]
>>> print(a)
[1, 2, 3]
```

You can access the elements of a list using an index. The indices start at 0, so to access the first element of the list, you would use the index 0:

Code 2.28 Illustration of List with index in Python

```
>>> a = [1, 2, 3]
>>> print(a[0])
1
```

You can also use negative indices, which count backward from the end of the list. For example, the index -1 refers to the last element of the list:

Code 2.29 Illustration of List with negative index in Python

```
>>> a = [1, 2, 3]
>>> print(a[-1])
3
```

You can also use slicing to access a range of elements in a list. For example:

Code 2.30 Illustration of List with slicing in Python

```
>>> a = [1, 2, 3, 4, 5]
>>> print(a[1:3])
[2, 3]
```

This will return a new list with elements at indices 1 and 2 (i.e., 2 and 3). Slice a[1:3] does not include the element at index 3. If you want to include the element at index 3, you can use slice a[1:4].

2.9.5 Tuples

In Python, a tuple is an immutable sequence type. Tuples are similar to lists, but they are created using parentheses instead of square brackets. Because tuples are immutable, you can't add or remove elements from them or sort them in place. However, you can use tuples to create new tuples, by concatenating or slicing them. Here's an example of how to create a tuple.

Code 2.30 Illustration of tuple in Python

```
>>> t = (1, 'a', 3.14)
>>> print(t)
(1, 'a', 3.14)
```

You can access the elements of a tuple using indexing, just like with a list:

```
>>> t[1]
'a
```

You can also slice a tuple, to get a new tuple with only a portion of the original tuple:

```
>>> t[1:]
('a', 3.14)
```

Tuples also support all of the common sequence operations, such as concatenation, repetition, and membership testing.

Code 2.31 Illustration of tuple in Python

```
>>> t * 3
(1, 'a', 3.14, 1, 'a', 3.14, 1, 'a', 3.14)
>>> 3 in t
False
>>> t + (4, 5, 6)
(1, 'a', 3.14, 4, 5, 6)
```

Because tuples are immutable, you can be sure that the values in the tuple won't be changed accidentally.

2.9.6 Sets

In Python, a set is a collection of items that is unordered, changeable, and does not allow duplicates. Sets are written with curly braces, and the elements are separated by commas. Here's an example of how to create a set in Python:

Code 2.32 Illustration of set in Python

```
# Create a set
fruits = {'apple', 'banana', 'mango'}
# Check the type of the object
print(type(fruits))
# Output: <class 'set'>
```

Sets are useful for storing and working with data when you don't need to preserve the order of the items, or when you want to eliminate duplicates. For example, you might use a set to store a list of unique words in a document or to store a list of unique user IDs in a database. You can perform various operations on sets, such as adding and removing items, computing the intersection and union of sets, and so on. Here are some examples:

Code 2.33 Illustration of set in Python

```
# Add an element to the set
fruits.add('orange')
print(fruits)
# Output: {'apple', 'banana', 'mango', 'orange'}

# Remove an element from the set
fruits.remove('banana')
print(fruits)
# Output: {'apple', 'mango', 'orange'}

# Compute the intersection of two sets
set1 = {1, 2, 3, 4}
set2 = {3, 4, 5, 6}
intersection = set1 & set2
print(intersection)
# Output: {3, 4}

# Compute the union of two sets
set1 = {1, 2, 3, 4}
set2 = {3, 4, 5, 6}
union = set1 | set2
print(union)
# Output: {1, 2, 3, 4, 5, 6}
```

2.7.8 Dictionaries

In Python, a dictionary is a collection of key-value pairs. It is an unordered data structure that allows you to store and access data efficiently. Here is an example of how you can create a dictionary in Python:

Code 2.34 Illustration of dictionary in Python

```
>>> my_dict = {'a': 1, 'b': 2, 'c': 3}
>>> print(my_dict)
{'a': 1, 'b': 2, 'c': 3}
You can access the values in a dictionary by using the keys:
>>> my_dict = {'a': 1, 'b': 2, 'c': 3}
>>> print(my_dict['a'])
1
>>> print(my_dict['b'])
2
>>> print(my_dict['c'])
3
```

You can also use the get() method to access the values in a dictionary. This method returns the value for the given key if it exists in the dictionary. If the key does not exist, it returns a default value:

Code 2.35 Illustration of dictionary in Python

```
>>> my_dict = {'a': 1, 'b': 2, 'c': 3}
>>> print(my_dict.get('a'))
1
>>> print(my_dict.get('d'))
None
>>> print(my_dict.get('d', 'key does not exist'))
'key does not exist'
>>> my_dict = {'a': 1, 'b': 2, 'c': 3}
>>> print(my_dict.get('a'))
1
>>> print(my_dict.get('d'))
None
>>> print(my_dict.get('d', 'key does not exist'))
'key does not exist'
```

You can modify the values in a dictionary by using the keys:

Code 2.36 Illustration of dictionary in Python

```
>>> my_dict = {'a': 1, 'b': 2, 'c': 3}
>>> my_dict['a'] = 10
>>> my_dict['b'] = 20
>>> my_dict['c'] = 30
>>> print(my_dict)
{'a': 10, 'b': 20, 'c': 30}
```

You can add new key-value pairs to a dictionary using the same syntax:

Code 2.36 Illustration of dictionary in Python

```
>>> my_dict = {'a': 1, 'b': 2, 'c': 3}
>>> my_dict['d'] = 4
>>> print(my_dict)
{'a': 1, 'b': 2, 'c': 3, 'd': 4}
```

You can also use the del statement to remove a key-value pair from a dictionary:

Code 2.37 Illustration of dictionary in Python

```
>>> my_dict = {'a': 1, 'b': 2, 'c': 3}
>>> del my_dict['b']
>>> print(my_dict)
{'a': 1, 'c': 3}
```

Finally, you can use the clear() method to remove all key-value pairs from a dictionary:

Code 2.38 Illustration of dictionary in Python

```
>>> my_dict = {'a': 1, 'b': 2, 'c': 3}
>>> my_dict.clear()
>>> print(my_dict)
{}
```

2.10 Data Type Conversion

Data type conversion, also known as typecasting, is the process of converting a value from one data type to another. For example, converting an integer to a string, or a string to a floating-point number. This can be done using built-in functions or methods in most programming languages, such as int(), float(), str(), etc. It's important to be aware of the potential loss of precision or data that can occur during type conversion, especially when converting between different numeric tyIn many programming languages, there are built-in functions or methods that can be used to convert a value from one data type to another. These functions are typically named after the data type they convert to, and take the value to be converted as their input.

For example, in Python, the int() function can be used to convert a value to an integer. If the value is a string, it must contain a number that can be parsed as an integer. Otherwise, it will raise a ValueError. Similarly, the float() function can be used to convert a value to a floating-point number and str() function can be used to convert value to a string.

Here are some examples of data type conversion in Python:

Code 2.39 Illustration of data type conversion in Python

```
x = "123"
y = int(x) # y is now 123, an integer
z = 3.14
a = int(z) # a is now 3, an integer
b = "3.14"
c = float(b) # c is now 3.14, a floating-point number
```

It's important to be aware of the potential loss of precision or data that can occur during type conversion, especially when converting between different numeric types. For example, when converting a large integer to a floating-point number, the decimal places beyond the decimal point may be lost, resulting in an approximation of the original value.

There are two types of type conversion methods in Python:

- Implicit type conversion
- Explicit type conversion.

2.10.1 Implicit Type Conversion in Python

In Python, data type conversion can also be done implicitly, without the use of built-in functions or methods. Implicit data type conversion, also known as "type coercion," occurs when a value of one data type is used in an operation or expression with a value of a different data type. Python will automatically convert one of the values to the appropriate data type to allow the operation to proceed.

Code 2.40 Illustration of Implicit data type conversion in Python

```
x = 3
y = 2.5
z = x + y # z is now 5.5, a floating-point number
a = "Hello"
b = "world"
c = a + b # c is now "Helloworld", a string
```

In the first example, an integer (x) is added to a floating-point number (y) and the result is a floating-point number. In the second example, two strings (a and b) are concatenated and the result is a new string. It's important to be aware of the potential issues that can arise from implicit data type conversion, such as loss of precision or unexpected behavior in certain situations. It's good practice to explicitly convert data types when necessary, using built-in functions or methods, to ensure that the desired behavior is achieved.

2.10.2 Explicit Type Conversion in Python

Explicit type conversion, also known as "typecasting," is the process of explicitly converting a value from one data type to another using built-in functions or methods. Python provides several built-in functions to perform explicit type conversion such as int(), float(), str(), etc.

```
x = "abc"
y = int(x)
# This will raise a ValueError because the string "abc" cannot be parsed as an integer.
```

Explicit type conversion is a powerful feature that allows you to control the data type of a value and make sure that your code is handling data in the way you expect. It also improves the readability of the code and makes it easier to understand.

2.11 Input and output

In Python, there are several ways to accept input from the user and to provide output to the user. Here are some common ways to accept input in Python:

- **Using the input() function:** This function reads a line of text from the user. For example:

```
name = input("Enter your name: ")
print("Hello, " + name)
```

- **Using command line arguments:** When you run a Python script from the command line, you can pass in arguments after the script name. For example, if you have a script called myscript.py, you can run it with arguments like this: python myscript.py arg1 arg2. You can access the command line arguments in your Python script using the sys module. Here's an example of how to access the command line arguments in a script:

```
import sys
# Access the arguments using sys.argv
arg1 = sys.argv[1]
arg2 = sys.argv[2]
print("Argument 1:", arg1)
print("Argument 2:", arg2)
```

And here's an example of how you would run this script from the command line:

```
python myscript.py hello world
```

This would print the following output:

```
Argument 1: hello
Argument 2: world
```

There are other ways to accept input in Python, such as using the argparse module or reading from a file, but these are the most basic methods. To provide output to the user, you can use the print() function. For example:

```
print("Hello, world!")
```

This would print the string "Hello, world!" to the console.

2.12 Import

In Python, the import statement is used to import modules whose functions or variables can be used in your current program. For example, to import the math module, you can use the following code:

```
import math
```

This allows you to access the functions and variables defined in the math module using the dot notation. For example, you can use the sqrt() function from the math module like this:

Code 2.41 Illustration of import statement in Python

```
import math
x = math.sqrt(25)
print(x)  # Output: 5.0
```

You can also import specific functions or variables from a module using the from keyword. For example:

Code 2.42 Illustration of import statement in Python

```
from math import sqrt
x = sqrt(25)
print(x)  # Output: 5.0
```

2.13 Summary

In this chapter, we covered the fundamentals of the Python language, including keywords, identifiers, variables, and the rules for using them. We also discussed Python documentation, single-line and multi-line comments, and various data types such as numbers, strings, lists, tuples, sets, dictionaries, and files. We demonstrated how to use interactive input and output functions in Python and showed how to do formatted input and output. Finally, we demonstrated how to use the import command to call and use one module in another.

Review Questions

1. What are the Python keywords and how are they used in a program?
2. What is the difference between a Python identifier and a Python keyword?
3. How does identation affect the structure of a Python program?
4. What are some common Python statements used for flow control and iteration?
5. How does the input() function work in Python and what is its output data type?
6. What is the purpose of using documentation in a Python program and how is it written?
7. How does the import statement work in Python and what are the different types of imports?
8. What are the different ways to perform output operations in Python?
9. How can we handle errors and exceptions in Python programs and what are the built-in exception types?
10. What is the difference between a local and global variable in Python and when should each be used?
11. Which of the following is not a Python data type?
    a. list
    b. tuple
    c. dictionary
    d. Matrix
12. What is the data type of 'Hello, World!' in Python?
    a. int
    b. float
    c. string
    d. boolean

3

Operators and Expressions

Highlights

- All Python operators
- Precedence and associativity of operators
- Expressions

Python is a versatile and widely-used programming language that offers an array of operators to assist in carrying out a range of tasks. Its simplicity and readability make it an ideal choice for coders of all skill levels. Whether you are a beginner or a seasoned programmer, the utilization of Python operators can greatly enhance your coding abilities and improve your overall output. From basic arithmetic operators to logical operators, Python has everything you need to embark on your coding journey with confidence. With its vast libraries and frameworks, Python provides a comprehensive set of tools for developing complex algorithms, applications, and data analysis processes.

3.1 Operator

Operators in Python are special symbols that perform specific operations on one, two or more operands (values) and produce a result. Operators can be classified into different categories such as arithmetic, comparison, logical, bitwise, assignment and identity operators, each with a specific purpose.

- Arithmetic operators
- Comparison (Relational) operators
- Logical operators
- Boolean operators
- Assignment operators
- Bitwise operators
- Membership operators
- Identity operators

3.1.1 Arithmetic Operators

Arithmetic Operators are the basic mathematical operators in Python used to perform arithmetic operations such as addition, subtraction, multiplication, division, and others. These operators are represented by symbols such as +, -, *, /, %, and **. They are used to perform mathematical operations on numbers and produce a single output value. For example, addition (+) operator is used to add two values, subtraction (-) operator is used to subtract two values, and so on. With these operators, you can perform various mathematical calculations in Python, making it an ideal choice for numerical computing and data analysis. Additionally, Python provides support for complex numbers, which can be manipulated using arithmetic operators, making it a powerful tool for advanced mathematical and scientific calculations.

Table 3.1: Arithmetic Operators

Operator	Symbol	Description
Addition	+	Adds two values
Subtraction	-	Subtracts one value from another
Multiplication	*	Multiplies two values
Division	/	Divides one value by another (returns a float)
Floor Division	//	Divides one value by another and rounds down to the nearest integer
Modulus	%	Returns the remainder of a division operation
Exponent	**	Raises a value to a power

Code 3.1 Illustration of arithmetic operators

```
a = 5
b = 2
print(a + b)      # 7
print(a - b)      # 3
print(a * b)      # 10
print(a / b)   # 2.5
print(a // b)     # 2
print(a % b)    # 1
print(a ** b)   # 25
```

Let's see another examples:

Code 3.2 Illustration of arithmetic operators

```
# Addition
x = 3 + 4
print(x)  # Output: 7

# Subtraction
x = 3 - 4
print(x)  # Output: -1

# Multiplication
x = 3 * 4
print(x)  # Output: 12

# Division
x = 3 / 4
print(x) # Output: 0.75

# Modulus
x = 7 % 3
print(x)  # Output: 1
```

```
# Exponentiation
x = 3 ** 4
print(x)  # Output: 81

# Floor division
x = 7 // 3
print(x)  # Output: 2
```

It's also important to note that Python follows the order of operations (PEMDAS) when evaluating arithmetic expressions.

PEMDAS stands for Parentheses, Exponents, Multiplication and Division, and Addition and Subtraction. It is the order in which Python (and most other programming languages and math systems) evaluates arithmetic operations in an expression.

1. Parentheses: Expressions within parentheses are evaluated first.
2. Exponents: Exponentiation (ie raising to a power) is done next.
3. Multiplication and Division (from left to right): These operations are done next, from left to right.
4. Addition and Subtraction (from left to right): These operations are done last, from left to right.

3.1.2 Comparison Operators

Comparison operators are an essential part of any programming language, and Python is no exception. These operators allow you to compare values and determine the relationship between them. The result of a comparison is a Boolean value, either True or False, which can be used to make decisions in your code. In Python, the following comparison operators are available: "==" (equal to), "!=" (not equal to), ">" (greater than), "<" (less than), ">=" (greater than or equal to), and "<=" (less than or equal to). These operators can be used to compare numbers, strings, and even objects. It's important to note that the use of comparison operators is a fundamental aspect of programming and understanding how to use them correctly is crucial for writing effective and efficient code.

Table 3.2: comparison operators

Operator	Meaning	Example	Result
==	Equal to	3 == 2	False

Operator	Meaning	Example	Result
!=	Not equal to	3 != 2	True
>	Greater than	3 > 2	True
<	Less than	3 < 2	False
>=	Greater than or equal to	3 >= 2	True
<=	Less than or equal to	3 <= 2	False

These operators return a Boolean value (either True or False) depending on the result of the comparison. Here are some examples of how you can use these operators:

Code 3.3 Illustration of comparison operators

```
# Equal to
x = 3
y = 4
print(x == y) # Output: False

# Not equal to
x = 3
y = 4
print(x != y)  # Output: True

# Greater than
x = 3
y = 4
print(x > y)  # Output: False

# Less than
x = 3
y = 4
print(x < y)  # Output: True

# Greater than or equal to
x = 3
y = 4
print(x >= y)  # Output: False

# Less than or equal to
x = 3
y = 4
print(x <= y)  # Output: True
```

3.1.3 Assignment Operator

In Python, the assignment operator is the "=" symbol. It is used to assign a value to a variable. For example, in the statement "x = 5", the variable "x" is being assigned the value of 5. In addition to the basic assignment operator, there are a few other assignment operators that can be used to perform operations and assign the result to a variable in a single statement. For example:

Code 3.4 Illustration of assignment operator

```
x = 10
y = 5
z = x + y
```

In the above example, the variable x is assigned the value 10, y is assigned the value 5, and z is assigned the value of x + y, which is 15. Here is a table that summarizes the various assignment operators in Python, their corresponding functionality, and examples of their usage with the resulting value of the variable:

Table 3.3: Assignment operators

Operator	Meaning	Example	Result
=	Basic assignment: Assigns a value to a variable	x = 5	x = 5
+=	Add and assign: which adds the right-hand side to the variable on the left-hand side and assigns the result to the variable.	x += 5	x = x + 5
-=	Subtract and assign: which subtracts the right-hand side from the variable on the left-hand side and assigns the result to the variable.	x -= 5	x = x - 5
*=	Multiply and assign: which multiplies the variable on the left-hand side by the right-hand side and assigns the result to the variable	x *= 5	x = x * 5
/=	Divide and assign: which divides the variable on the left-hand side by the right-hand side and assigns the result to the variable.	x /= 5	x = x / 5
//=	Floor divide and assign: which performs floor division on the variable on the left-hand side by the right-hand side and assigns the result to the variable.	x //= 5	x = x // 5

Operator	Meaning	Example	Result
%=	Modulus and assign: which calculates the remainder of the variable on the left-hand side when divided by the right-hand side and assigns the result to the variable.	x %= 5	x = x % 5
**=	Exponent and assign: which raises the variable on the left-hand side to the power of the right-hand side and assigns the result to the variable.	x **= 5	x = x ** 5
&=	Bitwise and assign: which performs bitwise and operation on the variable on the left-hand side by the right-hand side and assigns the result to the variable.	x &= 5	x = x & 5
^=	Bitwise xor assign: which performs bitwise xor operation on the variable on the left-hand side by the right-hand side and assigns the result to the variable?	x ^= 5	x = x ^ 5
>>=	Bitwise right shift assign: which performs bitwise right shift operation on the variable on the left-hand side by the right-hand side and assigns the result to the variable	x >>= 5	x = x >> 5
<<=	Bitwise left shift assign: which performs bitwise left shift operation on the variable on the left-hand side by the right-hand side and assigns the result to the variable.	x <<= 5	x = x << 5

It is important to note that the right-hand side of the operator must be a valid expression that can be evaluated to a value. Also, the above table is meant to give you an idea of the operations being performed and the resulting values, but in practice, you would need to assign the values to the variable and then perform the operations.

3.1.4 Logical Operators

In Python, the logical operators are and, or, and not. These operators allow you to create boolean expressions, which evaluate to either True or False. The most common logical operators are given as follow:

and: returns True if both the expressions are true, otherwise False
or : returns True if at least one of the expressions is true, otherwise False.
not : returns True if the expression is false, otherwise False.

Here is an example of each operator:

Code 3.5 Illustration of and, or and not assignment operator

```
# and operator
if (x > 0) and (x < 10):
    print("x is a positive single-digit number.")
# or operator
if (x < 0) or (x > 10):
    print("x is a negative number or a number greater than 10.")
# not operator
if not (x == y):
    print("x is not equal to y.")
```

The and operator returns True if both the expressions on either side of it are True, and False otherwise.

The or operator returns True if either of the expressions on either side of it are True, and False otherwise.

The not operator negates the boolean value of the expression that follows it. So, if the expression is True, not will make it False, and if the expression is False, not operator will make it True.

Lets understand with an example that shows the results of different logical operations using the and, or, and not operators in Python in the table.

Table 3.4: logical operators

Expression	Result
True and True	True
True and False	False
False and False	False
True or True	True
True or False	True
False or False	False
not True	False
not False	True

You can also combine multiple logical operations in an expression, for example: We have two variables x and y as shown in table number.

Code 3.6 Illustration of logical operators

```
x = 5
y = 3
print((x > 2 and y > 3) or (x < 10 and y < 10))
# prints True
# (False or True) = True
```

Note that the and, or, and not keywords are used to perform logical operations in Python, as opposed to the symbols &, |, and ! commonly used in other programming languages.

3.1.5 Bitwise Operators

In Python, the bitwise operators are &, |, ^, ~, <<, and >>. These operators allow you to manipulate individual bits in an integer value. Let'see in table below the common bitwise operators in Python with an example of how they are used :

Table 3.5 bitwise operators

Operator	Name	Example	Result
&	AND	5 & 3	1
|	OR	5 | 3	7
^	XOR	5 ^ 3	6
~	NOT	~5	-6
<<	Left shift	5 << 2	20
>>	Right shift	5 >> 2	1

Here in above example,

5 in binary is 101 and 3 in binary is 011,hence result calculated as follow:

- 5 & 3 = 001 which is 1
- 5 | 3 = 111 which is 7
- 5 ^ 3 = 110 which is 6
- ~5 = -6 in decimal
- 5 << 2 = 10100 which is 20 in decimal
- 5 >> 2 = 001 which is 1 in decimal

Keep in mind that these operators only work on integers and the result is also an integer.

Here another example of each operator:

Code 3.7 Illustration of bitwise operators

```
# & operator (bitwise AND)
x = 0b10101010 # 170
y = 0b01010101 # 85
z = x & y # 0b00000000 = 0

# | operator (bitwise OR)
x = 0b10101010 # 170
y = 0b01010101 # 85
z = x | y # 0b11111111 = 255

# ^ operator (bitwise XOR)
x = 0b10101010 # 170
y = 0b01010101 # 85
z = x ^ y # 0b11111111 = 255

# ~ operator (bitwise NOT)
x = 0b10101010 # 170
y = ~x # -171

# << operator (left shift)
x = 0b10101010 # 170
y = x << 1 # 0b101010100 = 340

# >> operator (right shift)
x = 0b10101010 # 170
y = x >> 1 # 0b01010101 = 85
```

The & operator performs a bitwise AND operation on two integers. It compares each bit of the first integer to the corresponding bit of the second integer, and if both bits are 1, the corresponding result bit is set to 1. Otherwise, the corresponding result bit is set to 0.

The | operator performs a bitwise OR operation on two integers. It compares each bit of the first integer to the corresponding bit of the second integer, and if either bit is 1, the corresponding result bit is set to 1. Otherwise, the corresponding result bit is set to 0.

The ^ operator performs a bitwise XOR operation on two integers. It compares each bit of the first integer to the corresponding bit of the second integer, and if the bits are different, the corresponding result bit is set to 1. Otherwise, the corresponding result bit is set to 0.

The ~ operator is a bitwise NOT operator. It inverts all the bits of the integer that follows it, changing all the 0s to 1s and all the 1s to 0s.

The << operator shifts the bits of an integer value to the left by the number of places specified by the second operand. For example, if x is an integer value with n bits, and y is an integer value with m places, x << y is equivalent to x * 2**y.

The >> operator shifts the bits of an integer value to the right by the number of places specified by the second operand. For example, if x is an integer value with n bits, and y is an integer value with m places, x >> y is equivalent to x // 2**y.

3.1.6 Special Operators

Python language offers some special types of operators like the identity operator and the membership operator. These are described below under

3.1.6.1 Identity Operators

In Python, the identity operators are used to determining whether two objects are the same object. There are two identity operators:

- is: returns True if the objects are the same object, False otherwise
- is not: returns True if the objects are not the same object, False otherwise

Here's an example of how to use the identity operators:

Code 3.8 Illustration of special operators

```
x = [1, 2, 3]
y = [1, 2, 3]
z = x
```

```
# x and y are different objects
print(x is y)  # Output: False
# x and z are the same object
print(x is z)  # Output: True
# x and y are not the same object
print(x is not y)  # Output: True
# x and z are the same object
print(x is not z)  # Output: False
```

It's important to note that the identity operators check for object identity, not object equality. In other words, they check if two objects are the same object in memory, not if they have the same content. For example

Code 3.9 Illustration of identity operators

```
x = [1, 2, 3]
y = [1, 2, 3]

# x and y have the same content
print(x == y)  # Output: True

# x and y are different objects
print(x is y)  # Output: False
```

check if two objects have the same content, you should use the equality operator (==).

3.1.6.2 Membership Operators

In Python, the membership operators are in and not in. These operators are used to test whether a value is found within a sequence (such as a string, tuple, or list) or not. The operator in returns True if the value is found in the sequence and False if it is not. The operator not in returns True if the value is not found in the sequence and False if it is.

Here is an example of how to use the membership operators:

Code 3.10 Illustration of membership operators

```
>>> # Test if 'a' is in the string 'abc'
>>> 'a' in 'abc'
True
>>> # Test if 'd' is not in the string 'abc'
>>> 'd' not in 'abc'
True
>>> # Test if 1 is in the list [1, 2, 3]
>>> 1 in [1, 2, 3]
True
>>> # Test if 4 is not in the list [1, 2, 3]
>>> 4 not in [1, 2, 3]
True
```

You can also use the membership operators with variables:

Code 3.11 Illustration of membership operators

```
>>> # Assign a string to a variable
>>> s = 'abc'
>>> # Test if 'a' is in the string
>>> 'a' in s
True
>>> # Assign a list to a variable
>>> l = [1, 2, 3]
>>> # Test if 2 is in the list
>>> 2 in l
True
```

3.2 Expressions

Expressions are statements that can be evaluated to a value. In Python, an expression is a combination of values, variables, and operators that can be evaluated to a single value. For example, the expression 2 + 3 is a numerical expression that evaluates to the value 5. The expression "Hello, " + "World!" is a string expression that evaluates to the value "Hello, World!".

Expressions can be simple or complex and can include variables, functions, and other elements. Here are some examples of Python expressions:

- 2 + 3
- "Hello, " + "World!"
- len("Hello, World!")
- 2 * 3 + 5
- "Hello, " * 3

In Python, expressions can be used in a variety of contexts, such as in assignments, function calls, and as part of control structures like loops and conditional statements.

3.2.1 Python Operator Precedence

In Python, operator precedence determines the order in which operations are performed. Operators with higher precedence are performed before operators with lower precedence. For example, in the expression 4 + 5 * 2, the multiplication operation (*) has higher precedence than the addition operation (+), so the multiplication is done first and the result is added to 4. The expression is evaluated as 4 + (5 * 2), which is equal to 14.

Here is a list of the operators in Python, listed in order of decreasing precedence:

1. () Parentheses
2. ** Exponentiation (raise to the power)
3. ~ + - Unary plus and minus (method names for the + and - operators)
4. * / % // Multiply, divide, modulo and floor division
5. + - Addition and subtraction
6. >> << Right and left bitwise shift
7. & Bitwise 'AND'
8. ^ | Bitwise exclusive OR and regular OR
9. <= < > >= Comparison operators
10. == != Equality operators
11. = %= /= //= -= += *= **= Assignment operators
12. is is not Identity operators
13. in not in Membership operators
14. not or and Boolean NOT, OR, and AND

You can use parentheses to override the precedence and specify the order in which the operations should be performed. For example, in the expression (4 + 5) * 2, the parentheses indicate that the addition should be performed before the multiplication, so the expression is evaluated as (4 + 5) * 2, which is equal to 14.

3.2.2 Associativity

In Python, the associativity of an operator determines the order in which operations with the same precedence are performed. Most operators in Python are left-associative, which means that operations are performed from left to right.

For example, in the expression 2 + 3 - 4, the addition (+) and subtraction (-) operators have the same precedence, so they are performed from left to right. The expression is evaluated as (2 + 3) - 4, which is equal to 1.

However, some operators are right-associative. This means that operations are performed from right to left. The exponentiation operator (**) is an example of a right-associative operator in Python.

For example, in the expression 2 ** 3 ** 4, the exponentiation operator (**) has the same precedence, so it is performed from right to left. The expression is evaluated as 2 ** (3 ** 4), which is equal to 2 ** 81, or 43046721.

Here is a list of the operators in Python, along with their associativity:

Left-associative:

- + - Addition and subtraction
- * / % // Multiply, divide, modulo and floor division
- >> << Right and left bitwise shift
- & Bitwise 'AND'
- ^ | Bitwise exclusive OR and regular OR
- <= < > >= Comparison operators
- == != Equality operators
- = %= /= //= -= += *= **= Assignment operators
- is is not Identity operators
- in not in Membership operators
- not or and Boolean NOT, OR, and AND

Right-associative:

- ** Exponentiation (raise to the power)

3.2.3 Non-Associative Operators

In mathematics, a non-associative operator is an operator that does not satisfy the associative property. The associative property states that for any three values, the order in which the operator is applied to them does not matter. In other words, if we have the values a, b, and c, and an operator *, the following expression should always be true:

(a * b) * c = a * (b * c)

If this property does not hold, then the operator is non-associative.

Here are some examples of non-associative operators:

The division operator (/). For example, (3 / 4) / 5 is not equal to 3 / (4 / 5).

The subtraction operator (-). For example, (5 - 3) - 2 is not equal to 5 - (3 - 2).

It's important to note that non-associative operators can still be used to perform calculations, but you need to be careful about the order in which you apply them. The order in which you apply non-associative operators can change the result of the calculation.

3.3 Summary

In this chapter, we have learned about different operators such as arithmetic, comparison, logical, bitwise, special operators, identity, and membership operators available in the Python language. All the operators are described with appropriate examples of each. We have learned how operators and operands form an expression, which is the basic sentence of a programming language. The precedence decides which operator will be evaluated first and associativity decides how to evaluate an expression if two operators exhibit the same precedence. Finally, we have learned how Python language evaluates expressions.

Review Questions

1. What are the different types of operators available in Python?
2. Can you explain the precedence of operators in Python?
3. What is the associativity of the Python operators?

4. How do you use arithmetic operators in Python expressions?
5. Can you give an example of a Python expression that uses a comparison operator?
6. What are the logical operators in Python and how are they used in expressions?
7. How do you use the assignment operator in Python expressions?
8. Can you explain the use of the ternary operator in Python?
9. What is the difference between a Python expression and a statement?
10. Can you provide an example of a Python expression that uses multiple operators and nested expressions?
11. Which of the following is not a type of operator available in Python?
    (a) Arithmetic operators
    (b) Comparison operators
    (c) Logical operators
    (d) Email operators
12. What is the purpose of using the precedence of operators in Python?
    (a) To determine the order of evaluation in an expression
    (b) To determine the type of the operand in an expression
    (c) To determine the associativity of the operator
    (d) To determine the value of the expression

4 Control Structures

Highlights

- Python if, if else, if-elif-if statements
- Python while, for, infinite loop
- Python break, continue and pass statements

Control structures are blocks of code that allow a programmer to specify the flow of execution in a program. In Python, there are three main types of control structures: if statements, for loops, and while loops.

If statements allow the programmer to specify a condition, and if the condition is met, a block of code will be executed. If statements can also include optional "else" clauses, which will execute if the condition is not met.

For loops allow the programmer to iterate over a sequence of elements, such as a list or a string. The programmer can specify the variable to be used for each element in the sequence, and a block of code to be executed for each element.

While loops allow the programmer to specify a condition, and as long as the condition is met, a block of code will be executed. Care must be taken while loops, as it is easy to create an infinite loop if the condition is always met.

Control structures are an essential part of programming, as they allow the programmer to specify the order in which code is executed and to repeat certain actions.

4.1 Decision Making Statements

In Python, decision-making is achieved through the use of control statements. Control statements are blocks of code that allow you to specify the flow of your program.

There are two types of control statements in Python:

- Conditional statements: These statements allow you to specify different actions to be taken based on whether a condition is true or false. In Python, the most common conditional statement is the if statement.
- Loop statements: These statements allow you to execute a block of code multiple times. In Python, the most common loop statements are for and while loops.

The conditional statements available in Python are as following:

- if Statement
- if-else Statement
- if-elif-else Statement
- Nested if Statement

4.1.1 Python if Statement

The if statement is a control structure that allows you to specify a block of code to be executed if a certain condition is true. Here is the syntax of an if statement in Python:

```
if condition:
    # code block
```

Here is a flowchart that illustrates how the if statement works:

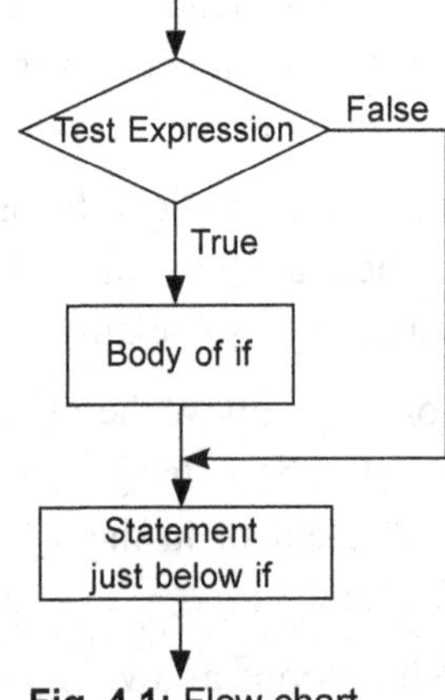

Fig. 4.1: Flow chart representing if statement

Here is an example of an if statement in Python that checks if a number is positive:

Code 4.1 A Python program to check whether the given number is positive.

```
num = 5
if num > 0:
    print("The number is positive")
```

The code block inside the if statement will only be executed if the condition num > 0 is true. In this case, the condition is true, so the code block will be executed and the message "The number is positive" will be printed to the console.

Another example of using an "if" statement to print multiple statements in Python:

Code 4.2 A Program to print multiple statements when a given condition is true.

```
x = 5
if x > 0:
    print("x is positive")
    print("x is greater than 0")
    print("x is a positive number")
```

In this example, the "if" statement is used to check if the variable x is greater than 0. If it is, the code inside the "if" block will be executed and all the three print statements will be executed, resulting in the following output:

```
x is positive
x is greater than 0
x is a positive number
```

4.1.2 Python if-else Statement

An if-else statement in Python is a control flow statement that allows you to execute different blocks of code depending on whether a condition is true or false.

The basic syntax of an if-else statement is as follows:

```
if condition:
    # code block to execute if condition is true
else:
    # code block to execute if condition is false
```

Here's a flowchart that illustrates the execution of an if-else statement:

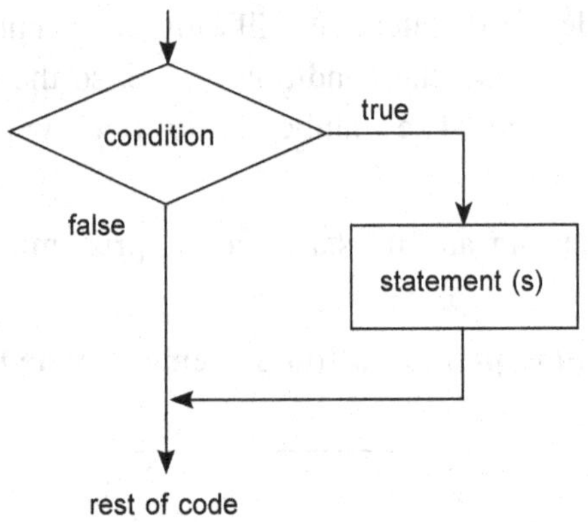

Fig. 4.2: Flow chart representing if-else statement

Here's an example of an if-else statement in Python that checks if a number is positive or negative:

Code 4.3 A Python program to check whether the given number is positive or negative.

```
number = 10
if number > 0:
    print("Positive")
else:
    print("Negative")
```

The output of this code would be "Positive". here's another example of using an "if-else" statement in Python where the input is taken from the user:

Code 4.4 A Program to check whether you are eligible to cast a vote or not.

```
age = int(input("Enter your age: "))
if age >= 18:
    print("You are eligible to vote.")
else:
    print("You are not eligible to vote.")
```

In this program, the input function is used to take the age of the user as an integer and store it in the variable "age". Then, the "if-else" statement is used to check if the variable "age" is greater than or equal to 18. If it is, the code inside the "if" block will be executed and the message **"You are eligible to vote."** will be printed. If the condition is not met, the code inside the "else" block will be executed and the message **"You are not eligible to vote."** will be printed.

4.1.3 Python if-elif-else

An if-elif-else statement is a control flow statement that allows a program to execute a specific block of code among multiple choices. It consists of a boolean expression for each if, Elif, and else clause, and a block of code to be executed if the boolean expression evaluates to True.

Here is the syntax for an if-elif-else statement:

```
if boolean_expression_1:
    # code block to be executed if boolean_expression_1 is True
elif boolean_expression_2:
    # code block to be executed if boolean_expression_2 is True
else:
    # code block to be executed if all boolean expressions are False
```

Here is a flow chart for an if-elif-else statement:

```
if boolean_expression_1:
    execute code block 1
else:
    if boolean_expression_2:
        execute code block 2
    else:
        execute code block 3
```

Here is an example program that demonstrates the use of an if-elif-else statement:

Code 4.5 A Program to check wether a given number is positive or negative using if-elif-else.

```
x = 10
if x < 0:
    print("x is a negative number")
elif x == 0:
    print("x is zero")
else:
    print("x is a positive number")
```

Output:

```
x is a positive number
```

In this example, the variable x is first given the value of 10. The program then checks if the value of x is less than 0. Since it is not, the program moves on to the next elif statement and checks if x is equal to 0. Since it is not, the program moves on to the final else statement and executes the code within it, which is to print "x is positive".

The if elif else statement allows you to check multiple conditions and execute different code for each one. The if statement checks the first condition, if the condition is true, it will execute the corresponding block of code and exit the statement. If the condition is false, the program will move on to the next elif statement and check the next condition. If none of the conditions are true, the code in the else block will be executed.

Code 4.6 A Program to demonstrate the use of multiple if elif conditions.

```
grade = "B"
if grade == "A":
    print("Excellent work!")
elif grade == "B":
    print("Good job!")
elif grade == "C":
    print("Average performance.")
elif grade == "D":
    print("Needs improvement.")
else:
    print("Invalid grade.")
```

In this example, the variable grade is assigned the value "B". The program then checks each elif statement in order, starting with the first one. When it finds the first condition that is true (grade == "B"), it will execute the corresponding block of code (printing "Good job!") and exit the statement. If none of the conditions are true, it will execute the code in the else statement, printing "Invalid grade."

You can see from the example, the if elif else statement is useful when you have multiple conditions that you want to check and different actions to take depending on the outcome of those checks.

4.1.4 Python Nested if Statements

Nested if statements allow you to include one or more if statements inside of another if statement. The syntax for a nested if statement is as follows:

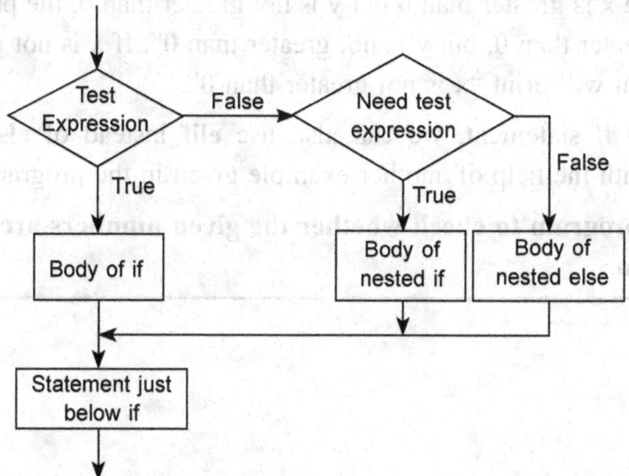

Here is an example of a nested if statement in Python:

Code 4.7 A program to demonstrate the use of nested if statement.

```
x = 10
y = 5

if x > y:
    print("x is greater than y")
   if x > 10:
      print("x is also greater than 10")
```

```
    else:
        print("x is not greater than 10")
else:
    print("x is not greater than y")
```

The output of this code would be:

```
x is greater than y
x is not greater than 10
```

In the above example, the outer if statement checks if the variable x is greater than 0. If it is, the inner if statement checks if the variable y is greater than 0. If both conditions are true, the program will print "Both x and y are greater than 0". If the x is greater than 0 but y is not greater than 0, the program will print "x is greater than 0, but y is not greater than 0". If x is not greater than 0, the program will print "x is not greater than 0".

In the nested if statement, we can also use **elif** instead of **else**: if. Let's understand with the help of another example given in the program below.

Code 4.8 A program to check whether the given numbers are greater or less than zero.

```
x = 5
y = 10

if x > 0:
    if y > 0:
        print("Both x and y are greater than 0")
    elif y<0:
        print("x is greater than 0, but y is less than 0")
else:
    print("x is not greater than 0")
```

4.2 Python Loops

In Python, a loop is a control structure that allows you to repeat a block of code a certain number of times or until a certain condition is met.

4.2.1 Types of Loops

- while loop
- Infinite loop
- for loop
- Nested loop

4.2.2 Python While Loop

A while loop in Python is used to execute a block of code repeatedly as long as a certain condition is True. The syntax for a while loop is as follows:

```
while condition:
    # code to be executed
```

The code inside the while loop will be executed repeatedly until the condition becomes False. It is important to make sure that the condition eventually becomes False, or the loop will run indefinitely, which is known as an infinite loop. Here is an example of a while loop in Python:

Code 4.9 A Program to print numbers from 0 to 9.

```
i = 0
while i < 10:
    print(i)
    i += 1
```

This while loop will print the numbers 0 through 9.

It is also possible to use a break statement inside a while loop to exit the loop early, or a continue statement to skip the remainder of the current iteration and move on to the next one.

```
i = 0
while True:
    if i == 5:
        break
    print(i)
    i += 1
```

This while loop will run indefinitely, but the break statement will cause it to exit when i becomes 5. The output will be the numbers 0 through 4.

```
i = 0
while True:
    i += 1
    if i % 2 == 0:
        continue
    print(i)
    if i == 10:
        break
```

This while loop will also run indefinitely, but the continue statement will cause it to skip the remainder of the current iteration when i is even, and the break statement will cause it to exit when i becomes 10. The output will be the odd numbers 1 through 9.

Here's another program that demonstrates the use of while loop in Python:

Code 4.10 Program to calculate the sum of numbers entered by the user.

```
# Initialize variables
sum = 0
number = 1
# Ask the user to enter numbers
while number != 0:
    number = int(input("Enter a number (0 to quit): "))
    sum = sum + number
# Print the result
print("The sum of the numbers is", sum)
```

Output:

```
Enter a number (0 to quit): 5
Enter a number (0 to quit): 10
Enter a number (0 to quit): 15
Enter a number (0 to quit): 0
The sum of the numbers is 30
```

In the above program, the while loop continues to execute as long as the value of the number is not equal to 0. The user is asked to enter a number, and the input is converted to an integer using int(). The entered number is then added to the sum of all previous numbers. When the user enters 0, the loop terminates, and the final result is printed.

4.2.3 The Infinite Loop

An infinite loop is a loop that runs indefinitely because the loop's condition is always True. This can occur if the condition is not updated inside the loop, or if the condition cannot be met. Here is an example of an infinite loop in Python:

```
while True:
    print("Hello, World!")
```

This loop will print "Hello, World!" indefinitely because the condition True is always True.This loop will keep printing the message "Hello, World!" until the program is interrupted. To interrupt the program, you can use **CTRL + C** in the terminal or **CTRL + Break** in the IDLE editor.

It is important to be careful when using while loops, as infinite loops can cause your program to crash or become unresponsive. To avoid infinite loops, make sure that the condition of the loop can eventually become False, or use a break statement to exit the loop when a certain condition is met.

```
i = 0
while True:
    print(i)
    i += 1
    if i == 10:
        break
```

In this example, the break statement causes the loop to exit when i becomes 10, preventing the loop from running indefinitely. The output will be the numbers 0 through 9.

4.2.4 Using else with while Loop

In Python, the else clause of a while loop can be used to specify a block of code that should be executed after the loop has finished executing, but only if the loop completed normally (i.e., if the loop was not exited prematurely by a break statement). Here is an example of using an else clause with a while loop in Python:

Code 4.11 A Program to demonstrate the use of else clause with a while loop.

```
i = 0
while i < 10:
    print(i)
    i += 1
else:
    print("Done!")
```

In this example, the while loop will print the numbers 0 through 9, and then the else clause will be executed, printing "Done!". If the while loop is exited prematurely by a break statement, the else clause will not be executed. For example

```
i = 0
while True:
    print(i)
    i += 1
    if i == 5:
        break
else:
    print("Done!")
```

In this example, the while loop will print the numbers 0 through 4, and then exit when i becomes 5. The else clause will not be executed.

The else clause of a while loop can be useful for executing clean-up code or for handling cases where the loop did not execute at all (e.g., if the loop's condition was False from the start).

4.2.5 Python for Loop

A for loop in Python is used to iterate over a sequence or an iterable object, such as a list, tuple, or string. The syntax for a for loop is as follows:

```
for item in iterable:
    # code to be executed
```

The for loop will iterate over the items in the iterable, and for each item, it will assign the value to the item variable and execute the code inside the loop. Here is an example of a for loop in Python that iterates over a list of numbers:

Code 4.12 A Program to demonstrate for loop in Python that iterates over a list of numbers.

```
for i in [1, 2, 3, 4, 5]:
    print(i)
```

This for loop will print the numbers 1 through 5. It is also possible to use a break statement inside a for loop to exit the loop early, or a continue statement to skip the remainder of the current iteration and move on to the next one.

```
for i in [1, 2, 3, 4, 5]:
    if i == 3:
        break
    print(i)
```

This for loop will print the numbers 1 and 2, and then exit when it encounters the number 3.

```
for i in [1, 2, 3, 4, 5]:
    if i % 2 == 0:
        continue
    print(i)
```

This for loop will print the odd numbers 1, 3, and 5, because the continue statement causes the loop to skip the remainder of the current iteration when i is even.

Code 4.13 A Program to print sum of all the numbers given in a list.

```
numbers = [1, 2, 3, 4, 5]
sum = 0
for num in numbers:
  sum += num
print("Sum of all numbers:", sum)
```

4.2.6 The range() Function

The range() function in Python is a built-in function that returns a sequence of numbers, starting from 0 by default, increments by 1 (also by default), and ends at a specified number. The syntax for the range() function is as follows:

```
range(stop)
range(start, stop[, step])
```

The stop parameter is required and specifies the end of the sequence. The start parameter is optional and specifies the starting number of the sequence. The step parameter is also optional and specifies the increment between each number in the sequence. Here are some examples of using the range() function:

Code 4.14 Illustration of range() function

```
# Print the numbers 0 through 9
for i in range(10):
    print(i)
# Print the numbers 2 through 9
for i in range(2, 10):
    print(i)
# Print the even numbers 0 through 8
for i in range(0, 10, 2):
    print(i)
# Print the odd numbers 1 through 9
for i in range(1, 10, 2):
    print(i)
```

The range() function is often used with a for loop to repeat a block of code a specific number of times. For example:

```
for i in range(5):
    print("Hello, World!")
```

This code will print "Hello, World!" 5 times.

Note that the range() function returns a sequence of numbers, but does not actually create a list. To create a list from a range(), you can use the list() function.

```
numbers = list(range(10))
print(numbers) # [0, 1, 2, 3, 4, 5, 6, 7, 8, 9]
```

4.2.7 For Loop with else

In Python, the else clause of a for loop can be used to specify a block of code that should be executed after the loop has finished executing, but only if the loop completed normally (i.e., if the loop was not exited prematurely by a break statement). Here is an example of using an else clause with a for loop in Python:

```
for i in [1, 2, 3, 4, 5]:
    print(i)
else:
    print("Done!")
```

In this example, the for loop will print the numbers 1 through 5, and then the else clause will be executed, printing "Done!". If the for loop is exited prematurely by a break statement, the else clause will not be executed. For example:

Code 4.15 break statement

```
for i in [1, 2, 3, 4, 5]:
    if i == 3:
        break
    print(i)
else:
    print("Done!")
```

In this example, the for loop will print the numbers 1 and 2, and then exit when it encounters the number 3. The else clause will not be executed.

The else clause of a for loop can be useful for executing clean-up code or for handling cases where the loop did not execute at all (e.g., if the iterable object is empty).

4.2.8 Nested Loops

It is possible to have loops inside of other loops in Python, known as nested loops. The inner loop will be executed completely for each iteration of the outer loop. Here is an example of a nested loop in Python:

Code 4.16 Illustration of nested loop

```
for i in range(1, 4):
    for j in range(1, 4):
        print(i, j)
```

This code will print the following:

```
1 1
1 2
1 3
2 1
2 2
2 3
3 1
3 2
3 3
```

The inner loop (the for loop with the variable j) will be executed completely for each iteration of the outer loop (the for loop with the variable i).

It is also possible to use a break statement inside a nested loop to exit both the inner loop and the outer loop, or a continue statement to skip the remainder of the current iteration of the inner loop and move on to the next one

```
for i in range(1, 4):
    for j in range(1, 4):
        if j == 2:
            break
        print(i, j)
```

This code will print the following:

```
1 1
2 1
3 1
```

The inner loop will exit when j becomes 2, causing the outer loop to move on to the next iteration.

```
for i in range(1, 4):
    for j in range(1, 4):
        if j == 2:
            continue
        print(i, j)
```

This code will print the following:

```
1 1
1 3
2 1
2 3
3 1
3 3
```

The inner loop will skip the remainder of the current iteration when j becomes 2, but the outer loop will continue running.

4.3 Python Control Statements

In python to control the flow of the program basically used control statements are:

- break Statement
- continue Statement
- pass Statement

4.3.1 Python Break Statement

The break statement in Python is used to exit a loop early before the loop's condition becomes False. When a break statement is encountered inside a loop, the loop is immediately terminated, and the program execution moves to the next statement after the loop. Here is an example of using a break statement in a for loop in Python:

Code 4.17 break statement in python

```
for i in range(10):
    if i == 5:
        break
    print(i)
```

This for loop will print the numbers 0 through 4, and then exit when i becomes 5. The output will be:

```
0
1
2
3
4
```

It is also possible to use a break statement inside a while loop:

```
i = 0
while True:
    print(i)
    i += 1
    if i == 5:
        break
```

This while loop will print the numbers 0 through 4, and then exit when i becomes 5. The output will be:

```
0
1
2
3
4
```

4.3.2 Python Continue Statement

In Python, the continue statement is used to skip the current iteration of a loop and move on to the next iteration. It is used to interrupt the normal flow of a loop and return control to the beginning of the loop, allowing the next iteration to begin.

Here is an example of how to use the continue statement in a for loop:

Code 4.18 Illustration of continue statement

```
for i in range(10):
    if i % 2 == 0:
        continue
    print(i)
```

The output of this code will be:

```
1
3
5
7
9
```

The continue statement is encountered when it is even, causing the current iteration to be skipped and control to be returned to the beginning of the loop. As a result, only the odd numbers from 1 to 9 are printed.

The continue statement can also be used in a while loop. In this case, it would cause the loop to skip the rest of the current iteration and move on to the next iteration, just as it does in a for loop.

```
i = 0
while i < 10:
    i += 1
    if i % 2 == 0:
        continue
    print(i)
```

This code will have the same output as the for loop example above.

4.3.3 Python Pass Statement

In Python, the pass statement is a null operation - it does nothing. It is used as a placeholder in code blocks where some action is required, but no action is necessary. For example, you might use the pass statement in an if statement when you have not yet decided what action to take:

```
if some_condition:
    pass
```

The pass statement can also be used in a for or while loop when you have not yet decided what to do in the loop body:

Code 4.19 Illustration of pass statement

```
for i in range(10):
    pass
```

```
i = 0
while i < 10:
    i += 1
    pass
```

In both of these examples, the loop will iterate the specified number of times, but no action will be taken in the loop body.

The pass statement is often used as a placeholder while writing code, allowing you to get the basic structure of a program in place before adding more detailed code. It is also used in code blocks where the syntax requires a statement, but no action is needed.

4.4 Summary

In this chapter, we learned about the control structures available in Python. These include decision-making statements such as “if,” “if else,” and “elif,” as well as looping constructs like “while” and “for.” We also covered features like “while loop with else” and “for loop with else,” as well as the “range()” function. Additionally, we discussed control statements like “break,” “continue,” and “pass,” and provided flow diagrams for each control structure.

Review Questions

1. What are control structures in Python and why are they used?
2. Can you explain the syntax and use of the Python if statement?
3. How does the if-else statement work in Python?
4. Can you provide an example of an if-elif-else statement in Python?
5. How does the while loop work in Python?
6. What is the for loop in Python and how is it used?
7. Can you give an example of an infinite loop in Python?
8. What is the purpose of the break statement in Python?
9. Can you explain the continue statement in Python and when to use it?
10. What is the function of the pass statement in Python control structures?
11. Which of the following statements is true about control structures in Python?

    (a) They are used to control the flow of program execution

    (b) They are used to define the structure of the program

    (c) They are used to declare variables and functions

    (d) They are used to print output to the console
12. What is the syntax of the Python if statement?

    (a) if condition { statements }

    (b) if { condition } (statements)

    (c) if (condition) { statements }

    (d) if condition : statements

5

Python Native Data Types

Highlights

- Python native data types
- Number
- List, Tuple, Set, Dictionary
- Strings

In Python, there are several built-in data types that can be used to store and manipulate data. These native data types include

1. **Numbers:** Python has two main number types, integers, and floating-point numbers. Integers are whole numbers, while floating-point numbers are numbers with decimal points.
2. **Strings:** Strings are sequences of characters, and they can be defined using single or double quotes.
3. **Lists:** Lists are ordered sequences of objects, and they are defined using square brackets. Lists are mutable, meaning that their elements can be changed.
4. **Tuples:** Tuples are similar to lists, but they are immutable, meaning that their elements cannot be modified once created. Tuples are defined using parentheses.
5. **Dictionaries:** Dictionaries are unordered collections of key-value pairs, and they are defined using curly braces.

6. **Sets:** Sets are unordered collections of unique elements, and they are defined using curly braces.
7. **Booleans:** Booleans are used to represent the values True and False.

In addition to these native data types, Python also has several additional data types available in its standard library, such as arrays and collections.

5.1 Numbers

In Python, there are several types of numbers that you can use in your code. These include:

1. **int (short for "integer"):** These are whole numbers, such as 1, 2, 3, 4, etc. They can be positive, negative, or zero.
2. **float (short for "floating point"):** These are numbers with a decimal point, such as 3.14, 2.71828, etc. They can also be positive, negative, or zero.
3. **complex:** These are complex numbers, which are numbers with both a real and imaginary component. The real component is a float and the imaginary component is a float multiplied by the imaginary unit j. For example, the complex number 3 + 2j has a real component of 3 and an imaginary component of 2.

In addition to these basic number types, Python also has a few additional types that are used for representing numbers in specific contexts. For example, the decimal module provides support for arbitrary-precision decimal arithmetic, and the fractions module provides support for rational number arithmetic.

You can perform various operations on numbers in Python, such as addition, subtraction, multiplication, division, etc. For example

```
x = 3  # x is an int
y = 2.5  # y is a float
z = x + y  # z is a float
```

You can also use the built-in abs() function to get the absolute value of a number, the pow() function to raise a number to a power, and the round() function to round a number to a specified number of decimal places.

5.1.1 Number Type Conversion

In Python, you can convert one number type to another using the built-in functions int(), float(), and complex(). For example, you can convert an int to a float like this:

```
x = 3
y = float(x)  # y is now a float with the value 3.0
```

You can also convert a float to an int by using the int() function, but keep in mind that this will truncate the decimal part of the float. For example,

```
x = 3.7
y = int(x)  # y is now an int with the value 3
```

You can convert a number to a complex type by using the complex() function. You can pass in two arguments to the function, the real part, and the imaginary part, separated by a + or - sign. For example

```
x = 3
y = 4
z = complex(x, y) # z is now a complex number with the value 3+4j
```

It's also possible to convert a string representation of a number to a number type using the int(), float(), and complex() functions. For example

```
x = "3.14"
y = float(x)  # y is now a float with the value 3.14
```

5.1.2 Python Mathematical Functions

There are many built-in mathematical functions in Python that are included in the math module. Here is a table of some of the most commonly used ones:

Table 5.1: mathematical functions

Function	Description
math.ceil(x)	Returns the smallest integer greater than or equal to x
math.floor(x)	Returns the largest integer less than or equal to x
math.exp(x)	Returns e raised to the power of x
math.log(x, base)	Returns the logarithm of x to the specified base (default is e)
math.log2(x)	Returns the base-2 logarithm of x
math.log10(x)	Returns the base-10 logarithm of x
math.pow(x, y)	Returns x raised to the power of y

Function	Description
math.sqrt(x)	Returns the square root of x
math.acos(x), math.asin(x), math.atan(x)	Returns the arc cosine, arc sine, arc tangent of x, respectively.
math.cos(x), math.sin(x), math.tan(x)	Returns the cosine, sine, tangent of x, respectively.
math.degrees(x)	Converts an angle from radians to degrees
math.radians(x)	Converts an angle from degrees to radians

Please note that some of the trigonometric functions math.acos, math.asin, math.atan, math.cos, math.sin, math.tan expect input angle in radian and the functions that converts degrees to radian and vice-versa math.degrees(x), math.radians(x) are also provided

There are many mathematical functions available in Python, some of which are built-in to the language, while others are part of the standard library, and still others are available through external libraries. Here's in table 5.1 is the example program that demonstrates some of the common built-in and standard library mathematical functions in Python:

Code 5.1 Illustration of mathematical functions

```
import math

# Built-in functions
print(abs(-5)) # Absolute value
print(pow(2, 3)) # Raise to a power
print(round(3.14159)) # Round to nearest integer

# math library functions
print(math.ceil(3.14159)) # Round up to nearest integer
print(math.floor(3.14159)) # Round down to nearest integer
print(math.sqrt(16)) # Square root
print(math.log10(100)) # Base-10 logarithm
print(math.sin(math.pi / 2)) # Sine of a value (in radians)
```

This program starts by importing the math library, which provides additional mathematical functions not included in the built-in functions. The program then demonstrates some of the built-in functions, such as abs(), which returns the absolute value of a number, pow(), which raises a number to a power, and round(), which rounds a number to the nearest integer. The program then demonstrates some of the functions available in the math library, such as ceil(), which rounds a number up to the nearest integer, floor(), which rounds a number down to the nearest integer, sqrt(), which returns the square root of a number, log10() which returns base-10 logarithm of number and sin() which returns the sine of a value (in radians).

Please note that this example is quite basic and Python offers a lot more mathematical functions with additional libraries like NumPy, SciPy and SymPy etc. These libraries provide additional functionality such as linear algebra, optimization, signal processing, etc.

5.1.3 Python Trigonometric Functions

Python provides several trigonometric functions that can be used to perform mathematical operations on angles. These functions are defined in the math module and include:

Table 5.2: trignometric functions

Function	Description
math.sin(x)	Returns the sine of x radians.
math.cos(x)	Returns the cosine of x radians.
math.tan(x)	Returns the tangent of x radians.
math.asin(x)	Returns the arc sine of x, in radians.
math.acos(x)	Returns the arc cosine of x, in radians.
math.atan(x)	Returns the arc tangent of x, in radians.
math.atan2(y, x)	Returns the arc tangent of y/x, in radians.
math.sinh(x)	Returns the hyperbolic sine of x.
math.cosh(x)	Returns the hyperbolic cosine of x.
math.tanh(x)	Returns the hyperbolic tangent of x.
math.asinh(x)	Returns the inverse hyperbolic sine of x.
math.acosh(x)	Returns the inverse hyperbolic cosine of x.
math.atanh(x)	Returns the inverse hyperbolic tangent of x.

Here is an example of how you can use these functions in a Python script to compute the sine, cosine, and tangent of 30 degrees:

Code 5.2 Illustration of trigonometric functions

```
import math

# Convert 30 degrees to radians
x = math.radians(30)

# Compute the trigonometric functions
s = math.sin(x)
c = math.cos(x)
t = math.tan(x)

# Print the results
print("sin(30) =", s)
print("cos(30) =", c)
print("tan(30) =", t)
```

You can also use trigonometric functions in numpy. Here in code 5.3 is the example of numpy:

Code 5.3 Illustration of trigonometric functions in numpy

```
import numpy as np

# Convert 30 degrees to radians
x = np.deg2rad(30)

# Compute the trigonometric functions
s = np.sin(x)
c = np.cos(x)
t = np.tan(x)

# Print the results
print("sin(30) =", s)
print("cos(30) =", c)
print("tan(30) =", t)
```

The numpy module also provides a number of other useful mathematical functions, including functions for linear algebra, Fourier transforms, and probability distributions.

5.1.4 Python Random Number Functions

The random module in Python provides a number of functions for generating random numbers and selecting random elements from a list or other data structure. Here's a table of some of the most commonly used functions:

Table 5.3: random number functions

Function	Description
random.random()	Returns a random float between 0 and 1.
random.randint(a, b)	Returns a random integer between a and b (inclusive).
random.randrange(start, stop, step)	Returns a randomly selected element from range(start, stop, step)
random.uniform(a, b)	Returns a random float between a and b.
random.triangular(low, high, mode)	Return a random float in the range [low, high] where the mode argument defaults to the midpoint between the bounds, giving a symmetric distribution.
random.choice(sequence)	Selects a random element from a non-empty sequence.
random.choices(population, k=1)	Select k random elements from a given population with replacement
random.sample(population, k)	Select k unique random elements from a given population without replacement
random.shuffle(sequence)	Shuffles elements in a sequence in place.

Here's an example of how you can use some of these functions to generate random numbers:

Code 5.4: Illustration to random numbers

```
import random
# Generate a random float between 0 and 1
print(random.random())
# Generate a random integer between 1 and 10
print(random.randint(1, 10))
# Generate a random float between 2 and 4
print(random.uniform(2, 4))
```

```
# Select a random element from a list
my_list = [1, 2, 3, 4, 5]
print(random.choice(my_list))
#shuffle a list
print(random.shuffle(my_list))
print(my_list)
```

5.1.5 Python Mathematical Constants

The math module in Python provides several mathematical constants that you can use in your calculations. Here's a table of some of the most commonly used constants:

Table 5.4: mathematical functions

Constant	Value
math.pi	The mathematical constant pi (3.14159...)
math.e	The mathematical constant e (2.71828...)
math.inf	A positive infinity value
math.nan	A not-a-number value
math.tau	tau (2*pi) constant

Here's an example of how you can use these constants in a Python script:

Code 5.5: Illustration of python script

```
import math
# Compute the area of a circle with radius 2
radius = 2
area = math.pi * (radius ** 2)
print("Area of circle with radius 2:", area)
# Compute the value of e^2
e_squared = math.e ** 2
print("e^2:", e_squared)
# Compute the value of tau
tau_val = math.tau
print("tau:",tau_val)
```

5.2 Python Lists

The list is the most fundamental data structure in Python. Because the index of the first element of the list is zero, the index of the second element is one, and so on, the list is similar to an array in C, C++, or Java. The list, on the other hand, is a collection of disparate data elements. That is, a list can contain both numeric and character data.

Lists can be used to perform a variety of operations. Indexing, slicing, adding, multiplying, and checking for membership are some examples. In the following sections, we will illustrate all of these operations. Aside from that, the Python language has a number of built-in functions that we will go over.

5.2.1 Creating a List

In Python, a list is created by placing elements inside square brackets [ ] separated by commas. For example, to create a list of integers:

```
my_list = [1, 2, 3, 4, 5]
```

You can also create a list of strings:

```
my_list = ['a', 'b', 'c', 'd', 'e']
```

or a list of mixed data types:

```
my_list = [1, 'a', 3.14, True, [1, 2, 3]]
```

You can also create an empty list using the list() constructor or empty square brackets []

```
empty_list = []
empty_list = list()
```

5.2.2 Traversing a List

In Python, you can traverse a list using a for loop. Here is an example of how to use a for loop to print out each element in a list:

Code 5.6: Program to print each element of a list using for loop.

```
my_list = [1, 2, 3, 4, 5]
for element in my_list:
    print(element)
```

The above code will output:

```
1
2
3
4
5
```

You can also use while loop:

Code 5.7: Program to print element of a list using while loop.

```
my_list = [1, 2, 3, 4, 5]
i = 0
while i < len(my_list):
    print(my_list[i])
    i += 1
```

You can also use list comprehension to traverse the list:

Code 5.8: Program to traverse the element of a list.

```
my_list = [1, 2, 3, 4, 5]
[print(i) for i in my_list]
```

This will also output the same.

5.2.2.1 Indexing

In Python, indexing is used to access elements of a data structure, such as a list or string, by specifying a numerical position or index. The first element in a data structure has an index of 0, the second element has an index of 1, and so on. For example, to access the first element in a list called "mylist", you would use the code 5.9:

```
mylist[0]
```

You can also use slicing to access a range of elements in a data structure. The syntax for slicing is as follows:

```
mylist[start:end]
```

This will return a new list containing all elements from the start index (inclusive) to the end index (exclusive).

5.2.2.2 Traversing Nested Lists

Traversing nested lists in Python can be done using nested loops. A nested loop is a loop that is inside another loop. The outer loop iterates over the elements of the outer list, and the inner loop iterates over the elements of the inner list.

Code 5.9 Program to traverse a nested list using nested for loops:

```
nested_list = [[1, 2, 3], [4, 5, 6], [7, 8, 9]]
for sublist in nested_list:
    for element in sublist:
        print(element)
```

This code will print the elements of the nested list in order: 1, 2, 3, 4, 5, 6, 7, 8, 9.

Another way of traversing a nested list is using recursion. Recursion is a technique where a function calls itself. This can be used to traverse a nested list by recursing through each element of the list, until the base case is reached. Here is an example of traversing a nested list using recursion:

Code 5.10: Program to use of recursion for traversing a list.

```
def traverse(lst):
    for element in lst:
        if type(element) == list:
            traverse(element)
        else:
            print(element)
nested_list = [[1, 2, 3], [4, 5, 6], [7, 8, 9]]
traverse(nested_list)
```

This will also print the elements of the nested list in order: 1, 2, 3, 4, 5, 6, 7, 8, 9.

You can also use list comprehension to flatten the nested list and then iterate over the flattened list as shown in Code 5.13:

```
nested_list = [[1, 2, 3], [4, 5, 6], [7, 8, 9]]
flattened_list = [item for sublist in nested_list for item in sublist]
for element in flattened_list:
    print(element)
```

This will also print the elements of the nested list in order: 1, 2, 3, 4, 5, 6, 7, 8, 9.

5.2.2.3 Negative Indexing

In Python, negative indexing is a way to access elements of a data structure, such as a list or string, by specifying a negative numerical position or index. The last element in a data structure has an index of -1, the second to last element has an index of -2, and so on.

Positive Indexing

→

0	1	2	3	4	5	6	7	8	9
H	E	L	L	O	W	O	R	L	D
-11	-10	-9	-8	-7	-6	-5	-4	-3	-2

Negative Indexing

←

For example, to access the last element in "mylist", you would use the code:

```
mylist[-1]
```

Here is an example of using negative indexing to access the last element of a list:

Code 5.11: To access element from a list using negative indexing.

```
mylist = [1, 2, 3, 4, 5]
print(mylist[-1]) # Output: 5
```

Code 5.12: To access the second to last element of a string:

```
mystring = "hello"
print(mystring[-2]) # Output: "l"
```

You can also use negative indexing with slicing to access a range of elements in a data structure. For example, to get a sub-list of the second to last 3 elements in "mylist", you would use the code 5.13:

```
mylist[-3:-1] # Output: [3,4]
```

Negative indexing is useful when you want to access elements from the end of a data structure without knowing the exact size of the data structure. It can also make your code more readable by eliminating the need to subtract the size of the data structure from the index to find the corresponding element.

5.2.2.4 *Slicing*

In Python, "slicing" is a way to extract a portion of a sequence (e.g. a string, list, or tuple) by specifying two indices, a start index and an end index, separated by a colon. The slice will include all elements from the start index up to, but not including, the end index. For example, if we have a list called my_list, we can extract the second through fourth elements as shown in code 5.14 :

```
sub_list = my_list[1:4]
```

This will create a new list called sub_list that contains the elements at index 1, 2, and 3 of my_list. Negative indexing can also be used.

You can also specify a step with the slicing, like my_list[start:end:step]

Start: by default starts from 0 index.

End: last index of the element in the given range.

Step: to increment or decrement in list by given steps.

Also, you can slice a string using a similar approach.

```
sub_string = my_string[1:4]
```

This will create a new string called sub_string that contains the characters at index 1, 2, and 3 of my_string.

5.2.3 Changing or Adding Elements to a List

There are several ways to change or add elements to a list in Python.

Using the assignment operator =: You can change an existing element in a list by specifying its index and assigning a new value to it. For example

```
my_list[2] = 'new value'
```

Using the append() method: This method is used to add a new element to the end of a list. For example:

```
my_list.append('new element')
```

Using the insert() method: This method is used to add a new element at a specific index in a list. For example:

```
my_list.insert(2, 'new element')
```

Using the extend() method: This method is used to add multiple elements to a list. It takes an iterable as an argument and adds each element of that iterable to the list. For example:

```
my_list.extend([1, 2, 3])
```

Using the + operator: This operator can be used to concatenate two or more lists. For example:

```
new_list = my_list + [4, 5, 6]
```

Using the * operator: This operator can be used to duplicate a list a certain number of times. For example:

```
new_list = my_list * 3
```

Note that all of these methods except the assignment operator will modify the original list, while the assignment operator creates a new list.

5.2.4 List Methods

In Python, a list is a built-in data type that has a number of useful built-in methods for working with its elements. Here are some commonly used list methods:

Table 5.5 : List of methods

Method	Description	Modifies Original List	Returns
append(element)	Adds an element to the end of the list	Yes	None
extend(iterable)	Adds all the elements from an iterable to the end of the list	Yes	None
insert(index, element)	Inserts an element at a specific index in the list	Yes	None
remove(element)	Removes the first occurrence of the specified element from the list	Yes	None
pop(index)	Removes and returns the element at the specified index	Yes	The removed element
index(element)	Returns the index of the first occurrence of the specified element in the list	No	The index of the element
count(element)	Returns the number of times the specified element appears in the list	No	The count of the element
sort()	Sorts the elements of the list in ascending order	Yes	None

Method	Description	Modifies Original List	Returns
reverse()	Reverses the order of the elements in the list	Yes	None
clear()	Removes all elements from the list	Yes	None
copy()	Returns a shallow copy of the list	No	A new list
deepcopy()	Returns a deep copy of the list	No	A new list
len()	Returns the number of elements in the list	No	The length of the list
min()	Returns the smallest element in the list	No	The minimum element
max()	Returns the largest element in the list	No	The maximum element
sum()	Returns the sum of all elements in the list	No	The sum of the elements

5.2.5 List Functions

Here is a table that summarizes some of the commonly used list functions in Python:

Table 5.6 : List of functions

Function	Description	Returns
len(list)	Returns the number of elements in the list	The length of the list
max(list)	Returns the largest element in the list	The maximum element
min(list)	Returns the smallest element in the list	The minimum element
sum(list)	Returns the sum of all elements in the list	The sum of the elements
sorted(list)	Returns the sorted copy of the list	A new sorted list
reversed(list)	Returns the iterator of the reversed copy of the list	A iterator of the reversed list
enumerate(list)	Returns an enumerate object, containing the index and value of the list	An enumerate object

Function	Description	Returns
zip(list1, list2, ...)	Returns an iterator of tuples, where the i-th tuple contains the i-th element from each of the input lists.	An iterator of tuples
filter(function, iterable)	Returns an iterator from elements of iterable for which the function returns true.	An iterator
map(function, iterable)	Applies function to all items of iterable and returns an iterator of the results.	An iterator

5.2.6 List Comprehension

List comprehension is a concise way to create a new list in Python. Here is a table that explains the syntax and usage of list comprehension:

Table 5.7 : List comprehension

Syntax	Description	Example
[expression for item in iterable]	Creates a new list by applying the expression to each item in the iterable	[x**2 for x in range(10)] creates a new list containing the squares of numbers 0-9
[expression for item in iterable if condition]	Creates a new list by applying the expression to each item in the iterable that satisfies the condition	[x**2 for x in range(10) if x % 2 == 0] creates a new list containing the squares of even numbers 0-9
[expression for item1 in iterable1 for item2 in iterable2]	Creates a new list by applying the expression to each item in the iterable1 and iterable2	[x*y for x in range(3) for y in range(3)] creates a new list containing the product of every combination of numbers 0-2

List comprehension can be a useful tool when you need to create a new list based on some existing data or logic. It allows you to write more readable and efficient code, as it eliminates the need for explicit loops and temporary variables.

Note that list comprehension is not always the best choice, if the comprehension becomes too complex it might be better to use a for loop.

5.2.7 List Membership Test

In Python, you can use the in keyword to test if an element is present in a list. The membership test returns True if the element is in the list, and False otherwise. For example:

Code 5.18: To check whether given number exists in list or not.

```
my_list = [1, 2, 3, 4, 5]
print(3 in my_list) # True
print(6 in my_list) # False
```

You can also use not in to test if an element is not present in a list:

```
print(6 not in my_list) # True
```

You can also use any() function with a generator expression to check if any of the elements in the list satisfy a certain condition.

```
numbers = [1,2,3,4,5,6]
result = any(x>4 for x in numbers)
print(result) # True
```

You can also use all() functions with a generator expression to check if all of the elements in the list satisfy a certain condition.

```
result = all(x>0 for x in numbers)
print(result) # True
```

Keep in mind that the membership test is generally faster for lists than for other iterable types, like sets or tuples, because lists are ordered and have a specific index for each element.

Also, if you are trying to find out the existence of elements in a large list, using sets is more efficient than using lists.

5.3 Python Tuples

In Python, a tuple is a collection of ordered, immutable elements. Tuples are defined using parentheses, with elements separated by commas. For example, a tuple containing the integers 1, 2, and 3 would be written as (1, 2, 3). Tuples can contain elements of different types, such as integers, strings, and other objects. Because tuples are immutable, their elements cannot be modified once they are created. However, elements within a tuple can be accessed by their index, just like a list. Tuples are often used to store related pieces of data, such as a name and an age.

5.3.1 Creating a Tuple

In Python, a tuple can be created by placing elements inside parentheses, separated by commas. For example:

Code 5.19: Illustration of creating a tuple

```
# Creating a tuple with 3 elements
my_tuple = (1, "hello", 3.14)
# Creating a tuple with 2 elements
my_tuple2 = ("apple", "banana")
# Creating an empty tuple
my_empty_tuple = ()
```

You can also create a tuple without using parentheses by using a trailing comma. For example:

```
# Creating a tuple with one element
my_tuple3 = "apple",
```

It's also possible to create a tuple from a list or another iterable using the tuple() function:

Code.5.20: Illustration of tuple from list

```
# Creating a tuple from a list
my_list = [1, 2, 3]
my_tuple4 = tuple(my_list)
# Creating a tuple from a string
my_string = "hello"
my_tuple5 = tuple(my_string)
```

You can also use the * operator to unpack the elements of an iterable into a new tuple. As shown in Code 5.21 below:

```
# Unpacking elements of a list into a tuple
my_list = [1, 2, 3]
my_tuple6 = *my_list
```

As you can see, creating a tuple in Python is quite simple and straightforward. The key thing to remember is that tuples are collections of ordered and immutable elements, and are defined using parentheses and separated by commas.

5.3.2 Unpacking Tuple

To unpack a tuple in a program, you can use the assignment operator (=) in combination with multiple variables. The number of variables on the left side of the operator must match the number of elements in the tuple.

For example, if you have the tuple (1, 2, 3), you can unpack it into separate variables like this:

```
a, b, c = (1, 2, 3)
```

Now the variable a will contain the value 1, b will contain the value 2, and c will contain the value 3.

You can also use the tuple unpacking feature in a for loop to iterate through the elements of the tuple:

Code 5.22: Illustration of unpacking tuple

```
my_tuple = (1, 2, 3)
for element in my_tuple:
    print(element)
```

This will output:

```
1
2
3
```

You can also use * operator to unpack remaining items in the tuple:

```
a, *b = (1, 2, 3, 4, 5)
```

Now, a=1, b=[2, 3, 4, 5]

5.3.3 Traversing Elements in a Tuple

There are several ways to traverse the elements in a tuple:

1. **Using a for loop:** You can use a for loop to iterate through the elements in a tuple. For example:

```
my_tuple = (1, 2, 3)
for element in my_tuple:
    print(element)
```

2. **Using the tuple() function:** The tuple() function allows you to access the elements of a tuple by index. For example:

```
my_tuple = (1, 2, 3)
for i in range(len(my_tuple)):
    print(my_tuple[i])
```

3. **Using the enumerate() function:** The enumerate() function allows you to access both the index and the value of each element in a tuple. For example:

```
my_tuple = (1, 2, 3)
for index, value in enumerate(my_tuple):
    print(index, value)
```

4. **Using list comprehension :**

```
my_tuple = (1, 2, 3)
[print(i) for i in my_tuple]
```

All the above code snippet will output:

```
1
2
3
```

Note that, Tuple are immutable so you can not change any element of tuple, but you can traverse it.

5.3.3.1 Indexing

In Python, indexing refers to the process of accessing individual elements of a data structure, such as a list, tuple, or string. These data structures are indexed using square brackets [], with the index starting at 0 for the first element. For example, if you have a list of numbers called "numbers" and you want to access the first element, you would use the following syntax:

```
numbers[0]
```

5.3.3.2 Negative Indexing

In Python, negative indexing allows you to access elements in a list or array by counting from the end of the list or array, rather than the beginning. For example, if you have a list called my_list and you want to access the last element of the list, you can use the index -1 to do so: my_list[-1]. Similarly, you can use -2 to access the second to last element, -3 to access the third to last element, and so on.

5.3.3.3 Tuple Slicing

In Python, tuple slicing allows you to access a range of elements in a tuple by specifying a start and stop index, separated by a colon. For example, if you have a tuple called my_tuple and you want to access the second and third elements of the tuple, you can use the slice my_tuple[1:3]. This will return a new tuple containing the second and third elements of the original tuple.

Code 5.23: A program that demonstrates tuple slicing in Python:

```
# Define a tuple
my_tuple = (1, 2, 3, 4, 5)

# Use tuple slicing to access a range of elements
sliced_tuple = my_tuple[1:4]
print(sliced_tuple) # Output: (2, 3, 4)

# Use negative indexing with tuple slicing
sliced_tuple = my_tuple[-4:-1]
print(sliced_tuple) # Output: (2, 3, 4)

# Use step value in tuple slicing
sliced_tuple = my_tuple[1:5:2]
print(sliced_tuple) # Output: (2, 4)
```

In this example, we first define a tuple my_tuple containing the elements 1, 2, 3, 4, and 5. Then we use tuple slicing to access a range of elements by specifying a start and stop index. We also use negative indexing with tuple slicing and step value in tuple slicing to get desired output.

5.3.3.4 Changing/Updating a Tuple

In Python, tuples are immutable, which means that their elements cannot be modified once they are created. However, you can create a new tuple with the desired elements, and then reassign it to the same variable, effectively updating the tuple. For example, if you want to change the second element of a tuple called my_tuple from 2 to 10, you would create a new tuple with the desired elements, and then reassign it to my_tuple as shown in Code 5.30:

Code 5.24: updating a tuple

```
# Define a tuple
my_tuple = (1, 2, 3, 4, 5)

# Create a new tuple with the desired elements
new_tuple = list(my_tuple)
new_tuple[1] = 10
new_tuple = tuple(new_tuple)

# Reassign the new tuple to the same variable
my_tuple = new_tuple
print(my_tuple) # Output: (1, 10, 3, 4, 5)
```

Another way to change/update a tuple is shown in code 5.24 by converting it to list and then updating and again converting it back to tuple.

Code 5.25: Illustration of updating a tuple

```
# Define a tuple
my_tuple = (1, 2, 3, 4, 5)

# Convert the tuple to a list
my_list = list(my_tuple)

# Update the list
my_list[1] = 10

# Convert the list back to a tuple
my_tuple = tuple(my_list)
print(my_tuple) # Output: (1, 10, 3, 4, 5)
```

It's important to note that both these methods create a new tuple and reassign it to the same variable, but the original tuple remains unchanged.

5.3.3.5 Deleting a Tuple

In Python, you can delete a tuple by using the del statement and specifying the tuple variable that you want to delete. For example, if you have a tuple called my_tuple and you want to delete it, you can use the following code 5.32:

```
my_tuple = (1, 2, 3, 4, 5)
del my_tuple

print(my_tuple) # Output: NameError: name 'my_tuple' is not defined
```

As you can see, after the tuple is deleted, trying to access it will result in a "NameError: name 'my_tuple' is not defined" because my_tuple variable no longer exists.

It's important to note that once a tuple is deleted, it cannot be accessed or used again. Also, deleting a tuple does not remove its elements from memory, only the variable that refers to the tuple is deleted.

5.3.3.6 Python Tuple Methods

Here is a table that lists some of the most commonly used Python tuple methods along with their descriptions:

Table 5.8: Python tuple methods

Method	Description
count()	Returns the number of occurrences of a specific element in the tuple
index()	Returns the index of the first occurrence of a specific element in the tuple
len()	Returns the number of elements in the tuple
tuple()	Returns a tuple version of an iterable object

Note that this is not an exhaustive list of tuple methods, there are more methods that can be used with tuples like max(), min(), sorted() etc. You can check the python documentation for more details.

5.3.3.7 Python Tuple Functions

Table 5.9: Python tuple methods

Function	Description
all()	Returns True if all elements in the tuple are true, False otherwise
any()	Returns True if at least one element in the tuple is true, False otherwise
enumerate()	Returns an enumerate object that contains the index and value of each element in the tuple
filter()	Returns an iterator from elements of an iterable for which a function returns true
len()	Returns the number of elements in the tuple
max()	Returns the largest element in the tuple
min()	Returns the smallest element in the tuple
sorted()	Returns a new sorted list from elements in the tuple

Please note that this is not an exhaustive list of tuple functions, there are more functions that can be used with tuples like zip(), map(), reduce() etc. You can check the python documentation for more details.

5.3.3.8 Advantages of Tuple

There are several advantages to using tuples in Python:

1. **Performance:** Tuples are faster than lists because they are immutable and require less memory.
2. **Immutable:** Because tuples are immutable, they are safe to use as keys in a dictionary or as elements of a set, whereas lists cannot be used as keys in a dictionary or as elements of a set.
3. **Safety:** Tuples provide a way to separate and store related data that should not be modified. For example, you can use a tuple to store the x and y coordinates of a point, and be sure that the values won't change accidentally.
4. **Readability:** Tuples can make code more readable by allowing you to group related data together. This makes it easy to understand the meaning of the data and what it represents.
5. **Easy to use:** Tuples are easy to create and use. They have a simple syntax and can be created with or without parentheses.

6. **Iterable:** Tuples are iterable which means you can iterate over the elements of a tuple using a for loop.
7. **Return multiple values:** Tuples can be used to return multiple values from a function, which is more efficient than using a data structure like a list or dictionary.

5.4 Python Sets

In Python, a set is a collection of unique elements. Sets are defined using curly braces {} or the set() function.

Code 5.26: To create a set in Python:

```
# Using curly braces
my_set = {1, 2, 3, 4, 5}

# Using the set() function
my_set = set([1, 2, 3, 4, 5])
```

Sets are unordered, which means that the elements in a set have no specific order. Sets are also mutable, which means that you can add, remove, and update elements in a set after it is created. For example, you can use the add() method to add an element to a set, the remove() method to remove an element from a set, and the update() method to add multiple elements to a set at once.

Sets also support mathematical set operations like union, intersection and difference.

Code 5.27: Illustration of union, intersection and difference

```
# Define two sets
set1 = {1, 2, 3}
set2 = {3, 4, 5}

# Union
print(set1.union(set2)) # Output: {1, 2, 3, 4, 5}

# Intersection
print(set1.intersection(set2)) # Output: {3}

# Difference
print(set1.difference(set2)) # Output: {1, 2}
```

It's important to note that sets do not allow duplicate values, if you try to add a duplicate value to a set, it will be ignored.

5.4.1 Creating a Set

In Python, a set is a collection of unique items. You can create a set using curly braces {} or the set() function. For example:

```
# Using curly braces
my_set = {1, 2, 3}

# Using the set() function
my_set = set([1, 2, 3])
```

You can also create a set from a list or other iterable by passing it as an argument to the set() function as given in code 5.36:

```
my_list = [1, 2, 3]
my_set = set(my_list)
```

5.4.2 Changing/Adding Elements to a Set

In Python, sets are mutable, meaning that elements can be added or removed from a set after it is created. To add an element to a set, use the add() method. For example:

```
my_set = {1, 2, 3}
my_set.add(4)
print(my_set)
```

This will add the element 4 to the set my_set.

To add multiple elements to a set at once, use the update() method. This method can take any iterable, such as a list or another set, as an argument. For example:

```
my_set = {1, 2, 3}
my_set.update([4, 5, 6])
print(my_set)
```

5.4.3 Removing Elements from a Set

To remove an element from a set, use the remove() method. If the element is not present in the set, a KeyError will be raised. For example:

```
my_set = {1, 2, 3}
my_set.remove(2)
print(my_set)
```

This will remove the element 2 from the set my_set.

Alternatively, you can use the discard() method to remove an element from a set. This method does not raise an error if the element is not present in the set.

```
my_set = {1, 2, 3}
my_set.discard(4)
print(my_set)
```

This will not raise any error, as 4 is not in the set my_set

5.4.4 Python Set Operations

In Python, sets are a built-in data type that can be used to store a collection of unique elements. The following are some common set operations that can be performed in Python:

1. **Union:** The union of two sets returns a new set that contains all the elements from both sets. The union operation is performed using the | operator or the union() method.
2. **Intersection:** The intersection of two sets returns a new set that contains only the elements that are common to both sets. The intersection operation is performed using the & operator or the intersection() method.
3. **Difference**: The difference of two sets returns a new set that contains the elements that are in the first set but not in the second set. The difference operation is performed using the - operator or the difference() method.
4. **Symmetric Difference:** The symmetric difference of two sets returns a new set that contains elements that are in either of the sets but not in both. The symmetric difference operation is performed using the ^ operator or the symmetric_difference() method.

5. **Subset:** To check if a set is a subset of another set, you can use the <= operator or the issubset() method.
5. **Superset:** To check if a set is a superset of another set, you can use the >= operator or the issuperset() method.

It's worth noting that all these set operations return a new set and the original sets remain unchanged.

5.4.4.1 Set Union

In Python, the union of two sets can be found using the union() method or the | operator. For example, given two sets A and B, the union can be found as follows:

```
A = {1, 2, 3}
B = {3, 4, 5}
C = A.union(B) # C = {1, 2, 3, 4, 5}
D = A | B # D = {1, 2, 3, 4, 5}
```

Both A.union(B) and A | B will return a new set that contains all the elements from both sets A and B, without duplicates.

5.4.4.2 Set Intersection

In Python, the intersection of two sets can be found using the intersection() method or the & operator. For example, given two sets A and B, the intersection can be found as follows:

```
A = {1, 2, 3}
B = {2, 3, 4}
C = A.intersection(B) # C = {2, 3}
D = A & B # D = {2, 3}
```

Both A.intersection(B) and A & B will return a new set that contains the elements that exist in both sets A and B.

5.4.4.3 Set Difference

In Python, the difference between two sets can be found using the difference() method or the - operator. For example, given two sets A and B, the difference between A and B can be found as follows:

Code 5.42:

```
A = {1, 2, 3}
B = {2, 3, 4}
C = A.difference(B) # C = {1}
D = A - B # D = {1}
```

Both A.difference(B) and A - B will return a new set that contains the elements that exist in set A but not in set B.

It's also worth mentioning Symmetric difference, it can be found using the symmetric_difference() method or the ^ operator. It returns a set of elements that is in either of the sets but not in both.

```
A = {1, 2, 3}
B = {2, 3, 4}
C = A.symmetric_difference(B) # C = {1, 4}
D = A ^ B # D = {1, 4}
```

5.4.4.4 Set Symmetric Difference

In Python, the symmetric difference of two sets can be found using the symmetric_difference() method or the "^" operator. For example, if A = {1, 2, 3} and B = {2, 3, 4}, you can find the symmetric difference of A and B using the following code 5.44:

```
A = {1, 2, 3}
B = {2, 3, 4}
# Using the symmetric_difference() method
symmetric_diff = A.symmetric_difference(B)
print(symmetric_diff) # output: {1, 4}
# Using the "^" operator
symmetric_diff = A ^ B
print(symmetric_diff) # output: {1, 4}
```

Both the symmetric_difference() method and the "^" operator will return a new set containing the symmetric difference of the two sets.

5.4.5 Python Set Methods

In Python, sets are built-in data structures that are used to store unique elements. Sets are mutable and unordered, and they are defined using curly braces {} or the built-in set() function. Here are some common methods that can be used with sets in Python:

- **add(element):** Adds an element to the set.
- **clear():** Removes all elements from the set.
- **copy():** Returns a shallow copy of the set.
- **difference(set):** Returns a set containing the elements that are only in the original set and not in the specified set.
- **difference_update(set):** Removes the elements that are in the specified set from the original set.
- **discard(element):** Removes an element from the set if it is present.
- **intersection(set):** Returns a set containing the elements that are common to both the original set and the specified set.
- **intersection_update(set):** Removes the elements that are not in the specified set from the original set.
- **isdisjoint(set)**: Returns True if the set has no elements in common with the specified set.
- **issubset(set):** Returns True if all elements of the set are in the specified set.
- **issuperset(set):** Returns True if all elements of the specified set are in the original set.
- **pop():** Removes and returns an arbitrary element from the set. If the set is empty, it raises a KeyError.
- **remove(element):** Removes an element from the set. If the element is not in the set, it raises a KeyError.
- **symmetric_difference(set):** Returns a set containing the elements that are in either the original set or the specified set, but not in both.
- **symmetric_difference_update(set):** Inserts the elements from the specified set that are not already in the original set, and removes the elements from the original set that are in the specified set.
- **union(set):** Returns a set containing all elements from the original set and the specified set.
- **update(set):** Adds the elements from the specified set to the original set.

Additionally, there are some other in-built methods available like len(), min(), max() etc.

You can use these methods to perform various operations on sets in Python. It's also worth noting that python set has also support of set comprehension, which allows you to create a new set using a single line of code.

5.4.6 The in Operator

In Python, the in operator is used to check if an element is present in a sequence, such as a list, tuple, set, or string. The in operator returns a Boolean value indicating whether the element is found in the sequence. For example, if you have a list of numbers called numbers and you want to check if the number 5 is in the list, you can use the in operator like shown in below.

```
numbers = [1, 2, 3, 4, 5]
if 5 in numbers:
    print("5 is in the list.")
```

5.4.7 Python Set Functions

In Python, the built-in set functions are used to perform various operations on sets, such as checking if all elements meet a certain condition, finding the number of elements in a set, or finding the maximum or minimum element in a set. These functions can be used on any iterable, which includes lists, tuples, and sets. Here are some examples of how you can use the built-in set functions in a Python program:

```
# using the all() function
numbers = {1, 2, 3, 4, 5}
if all(x > 0 for x in numbers):
    print("All numbers in the set are positive.")

# using the any() function
numbers = {1, 2, 3, 4, 5}
if any(x > 4 for x in numbers):
    print("There are numbers greater than 4 in the set.")
```

```
# using the len() function
numbers = {1, 2, 3, 4, 5}
print("The set has", len(numbers), "elements.")

# using the max() function
numbers = {1, 2, 3, 4, 5}
print("The largest element in the set is", max(numbers))

# using the min() function
numbers = {1, 2, 3, 4, 5}
print("The smallest element in the set is", min(numbers))
```

5.4.8 Frozen Sets

In Python, a frozen set is a built-in immutable set data type. This means that once a frozen set is created, its elements cannot be added, removed or modified. Frozen sets are defined using the frozenset() built-in function or by using curly braces with a 'f' prefix. A frozen set can be useful in situations where you want to use a set as a key in a dictionary or as an element in another set, but you don't want the set to be modified. Here's an example of how to create a frozen set:

```
# Creating a frozen set using the frozenset() function
fruits = frozenset(["apple", "banana", "cherry"])
print(fruits) # output: frozenset({'apple', 'banana', 'cherry'})

# Creating a frozen set using a set literal
fruits = f{'apple', 'banana', 'cherry'}
print(fruits) # output: frozenset({'apple', 'banana', 'cherry'})
```

As you can see, the output of the print statement is a frozenset object.

You can use the same set methods, such as union() and intersection() on frozen sets and also use the built-in set functions such as len(), min() and max() etc. Because frozen sets are immutable, you can't add or remove elements from them after they've been created, and you can't modify their elements either.

```
fruits.add("orange") # raises an error
fruits.remove("banana") # raises an error
fruits.clear() # raises an error
```

Frozen sets are useful in situations where you need a set that can be used as a key in a dictionary, or as an element in another set, but you don't want the set to be modified.

5.5 Python Dictionary

In Python, a dictionary is a built-in data structure that stores key-value pairs, where each key is unique. Dictionaries are mutable, which means that you can add, remove, or modify elements after the dictionary has been created.

5.5.1 Creating a Dictionary

Dictionaries are defined using curly braces {} or the built-in dict() function. Here's an example of how to create a dictionary:

```
# Creating a dictionary using curly braces
person = {"name": "John", "age": 30, "city": "New York"}

# Creating a dictionary using the dict() function
person = dict(name="John", age=30, city="New York")
```

In this example, the dictionary "person" contains three key-value pairs: "name" is the key and "John" is the value, "age" is the key and 30 is the value, and "city" is the key and "New York" is the value.

5.5.2 Accessing a Dictionary

In Python, a dictionary is a collection of key-value pairs, where each key is unique. To access a value in a dictionary, you can use the key in square brackets [] after the dictionary variable name. For example, if you have a dictionary called "my_dict" with a key "name" and a value "John", you can access the value like this:

```
my_value = my_dict["name"]
print(my_value) # Output: "John"
```

You can also use the get() method to access a value. This method takes a key as an argument and returns the value for that key if it exists in the dictionary, otherwise it returns None (or a default value if specified). For example:

```
my_value = my_dict.get("name")
print(my_value) # Output: "John"
```

If you want to check if a key is present in the dictionary or not, you can use the in keyword. For example:

```
if "name" in my_dict:
    print("name key found")
else:
    print("name key not found")
```

It will return "name key found"

5.5.3 Updating a Dictionary

In Python, you can update the values of a dictionary by using the key in square brackets [] after the dictionary variable name, and assigning a new value to it. For example, if you have a dictionary called "my_dict" with a key "name" and a value "John", you can update the value like this:

```
my_dict["name"] = "Bob"
print(my_dict) # Output: {"name": "Bob"}
```

You can also use the update() method to update multiple key-value pairs in a dictionary at once. This method takes another dictionary as an argument and adds its key-value pairs to the original dictionary. For example:

```
new_dict = {"age": 25, "gender": "male"}
my_dict.update(new_dict)
print(my_dict) # Output: {"name": "Bob", "age": 25, "gender": "male"}
```

```
my_dict["address"] = "NYC"
print(my_dict) # Output: {"name": "Bob", "age": 25, "gender": "male",
"address": "NYC"}
```

It will add the key "address" to the dictionary with value "NYC"

5.5.4 Removing or Deleting Elements of a Dictionary

In Python, you can remove or delete elements from a dictionary using the following methods:

1. **The del keyword:** You can use the del keyword to remove a specific key-value pair from a dictionary. For example:

```
del my_dict["name"]
print(my_dict) # Output: {"age": 25, "gender": "male"}
```

   This will remove the key-value pair with the key "name" from the dictionary "my_dict".

2. **The pop() method:** The pop() method removes a specific key-value pair from a dictionary and returns its value. If the key is not found in the dictionary, it raises a KeyError exception. For example:

```
value = my_dict.pop("age")
print(value) # Output: 25
print(my_dict) # Output: {"gender": "male"}
```

4. **The popitem() method:** The popitem() method removes and returns an arbitrary key-value pair from a dictionary. If the dictionary is empty, it raises a KeyError exception. For example:

```
item = my_dict.popitem()
print(item) # Output: ("gender", "male")
print(my_dict) # Output: {}
```

5. **The clear() method:** The clear() method removes all key-value pairs from a dictionary. For example:

```
my_dict.clear()
print(my_dict) # Output: {}
```

5.5.5 Python Dictionary Methods

Python's built-in dictionary data type provides several methods that can be used to manipulate dictionaries. Here are some of the most commonly used dictionary methods:

Method	Description
dict.clear()	Removes all items from the dictionary.
dict.copy()	Returns a shallow copy of the dictionary.

Method	Description
dict.fromkeys(seq[, value])	Returns a new dictionary with keys from the given sequence and all values set to the given value (defaults to None).
dict.get(key[, default])	Returns the value for key if key is in the dictionary, else default. If default is not given, it defaults to None, so that this method never raises a KeyError.
dict.items()	Returns a view object that displays a list of dictionary's (key, value) tuple pairs.
dict.keys()	Returns a view object that displays a list of all the keys in the dictionary.
dict.pop(key[, default])	Removes and returns the value for key if key is in the dictionary, else default. If default is not given and key is not in the dictionary, a KeyError is raised.
dict.popitem()	Remove and return an arbitrary (key, value) item pair from the dictionary. If the dictionary is empty, calling popitem() raises a KeyError.
dict. setdefault(key[, default])	If the key is in the dictionary, return its value. If not, insert a key with a value of default and return default. default defaults to None.
dict.update([other])	Update the dictionary with the key/value pairs from other, overwriting existing keys. If other is a dictionary, the key/value pairs are added to the dictionary. If other is an iterable of key/value pairs, the pairs are added to the dictionary. If other is a mapping, the mapping's keys must be new-style strings to be accepted as keys.
dict.values()	Returns a view object that displays a list of all the values in the dictionary.

5.5.6 Python Dictionary Membership Test

In Python, there are several ways to test for membership in a dictionary, which are:

1. **in operator:** You can use the in operator to check if a key is present in a dictionary. For example:

```
>>> d = {'a': 1, 'b': 2, 'c': 3}
>>> 'a' in d
True
>>> 'd' in d
False
```

2. **dict.keys() method:** You can use the keys() method of a dictionary to get a view of all the keys in the dictionary, which can be used to test for membership. For example:

```
>>> d = {'a': 1, 'b': 2, 'c': 3}
>>> 'a' in d.keys()
True
>>> 'd' in d.keys()
False
```

3. **dict.__contains__() method:** You can use the __contains__() method of a dictionary to check if a key is present in the dictionary. For example:

```
>>> d = {'a': 1, 'b': 2, 'c': 3}
>>> d.__contains__('a')
True
>>> d.__contains__('d')
False
```

in operator and keys() method is generally recommended for membership testing as they are more readable and easy to understand, contains method is also same as in operator but it is less readable.

5.5.7 Python Dictionary Functions

In addition to the methods that can be used to manipulate dictionaries, Python also provides several built-in functions that can be used to work with dictionaries.

Function	Description
len(dict)	Returns the number of items in the dictionary.
str(dict)	Returns a string representation of the dictionary.
type(variable)	Returns the type of the passed variable. If passed variable is dictionary then it will return dict.
sorted(dict)	Returns a sorted list of the keys in the dictionary.
dict(seq)	Creates a new dictionary from a list of key-value pairs.
zip(*iterables)	Returns an iterator of tuples, where the i-th tuple contains the i-th element from each of the argument sequences or iterables.

Function	Description
enumerate(iterable, start=0)	Returns an enumerate object. iterable must be a sequence, an iterator, or objects supporting the iteration protocol. The start parameter defaults to 0. The enumerate object yields pairs containing a count (from start which defaults to 0) and a value yielded by the iterable argument.
all(iterable)	Return True if all elements of the iterable are true. If the iterable is empty, return True. Equivalent to: def all(iterable): for element in iterable: if not element: return False return True
any(iterable)	Return True if any element of the iterable is true. If the iterable is empty, return False. Equivalent to: def any(iterable): for element in iterable: if element: return True return False

5.6 Python Strings

In Python, a string is a sequence of characters enclosed in quotes (either single or double). For example:

```
>>> s = "Hello, World!"
>>> s1 = 'Hello, World!'
```

Method	Description
str.capitalize()	Returns a copy of the string with its first character capitalized and the rest lowercase.
str.upper()	Returns a copy of the string in uppercase.
str.lower()	Returns a copy of the string in lowercase.
str.count(sub[, start[, end]])	Returns the number of non-overlapping occurrences of substring sub in the range [start, end]. Optional arguments start and end are interpreted as in slice notation.
str.find(sub[, start[, end]])	Returns the lowest index in the string where substring sub is found within the slice s[start:end]. Optional arguments start and end are interpreted as in slice notation. Return -1 if sub is not found.
str.replace(old, new[, count])	Returns a copy of the string with all occurrences of substring old replaced by new. If the optional argument count is given, only the first count occurrences are replaced.
str.split([sep[, maxsplit]])	Returns a list of the words in the string, using sep as the delimiter string. If maxsplit is given, at most maxsplit splits are done. If maxsplit is not specified or -1, then there is no limit on the number of splits.

Method	Description
str.join(iterable)	Use to concatenate any number of strings. All the strings have to be joined using the string on which this method is called.
str.strip([chars])	Returns a copy of the string with leading and trailing characters removed. If chars is not specified, it defaults to removing whitespace.
str.lstrip([chars])	Returns a copy of the string with leading characters removed. If chars is not specified, it defaults to removing whitespace.
str.rstrip([chars])	Returns a copy of the string with trailing characters removed. If chars is not specified, it defaults to removing whitespace.
str.isalpha()	Return true if all characters in the string are alphabetic and there is at least one character, false otherwise.
str.isalnum()	Return true if all characters in the string are alphanumeric and there is at least one character, false otherwise.

5.6.1 Creating a String in Python

Here is a single Python program that demonstrates several ways to create a string:

```
# Using single or double quotes
s = "Hello, World!"
s1 = 'Hello, World!'
print(s)
print(s1)

# Using the str() function
x = 123
y = 3.14
s2 = str(x)
s3 = str(y)
print(s2)
print(s3)
```

```
# Using string literals
s4 = """This is a
multiline string"""
print(s4)

# Using String Interpolation
name = "John"
age = 30
s5 = f"My name is {name} and I am {age} years old"
print(s5)

# Using bytes and bytearray
s6 = b'hello'
s7 = bytearray(b'hello')
print(s6)
print(s7)
```

This program creates five strings using different methods, first two by using single and double quotes, next two by using str() function , one by using string literals and last two by using bytes and bytes.

5.6.2 Accessing String Characters

Here is a single Python program that demonstrates several ways to access the characters of a string:

```
# Using indexing
s = "Hello, World!"
print(s[0]) # H
print(s[-1]) # !

# Using slicing
print(s[2:5]) # llo
```

```
# Using the for loop
for c in s:
    print(c)

# Using the while loop
i = 0
while i < len(s):
    print(s[i])
    i += 1

# Using the enumerate function
for index, character in enumerate(s):
    print("Index: ", index, " Character: ", character)
```

This program demonstrates several ways to access the characters of a string. The first method uses indexing to access individual characters. The second method uses slicing to access a range of characters. The third and fourth method uses for and while loop respectively to access all characters one by one. The last method uses the enumerate function to access the index and character at the same time.

Please note that string in python is immutable, which means the individual elements of the string cannot be changed once it is created.

5.6.3 Changing or Deleting String Characters

In Python, strings are immutable, which means that once a string is created, its characters cannot be changed or deleted. However, there are several ways to create a new string with the desired modifications. One way to do this is to create a new string by concatenating substrings, which can be created using slicing and string methods such as replace(). Another way is to use string formatting and template strings.

Here's a single Python program that demonstrates several ways to change or delete characters in a string:

```
# Creating a new string by concatenating substrings
s = "Hello, World!"
new_s = s[:5] + "Python" + s[11:]
print(new_s) # "Hello, Python!"

# Using the replace method
s = "Hello, World!"
new_s = s.replace("World", "Python")
print(new_s) # "Hello, Python!"

# Using string formatting
name = "John"
age = 30
new_s = "My name is %s and I am %d years old" % (name, age)
print(new_s) # "My name is John and I am 30 years old"

# Using template strings
name = "John"
age = 30
new_s = f"My name is {name} and I am {age} years old"
print(new_s) # "My name is John and I am 30 years old"
```

The first method creates a new string by concatenating substrings using slicing, which is obtained from the original string. The second method uses the replace() method to replace a specific substring with a new one. The third method uses string formatting to create a new string with placeholders filled with values. The last method uses template strings, which is a new feature introduced in Python 3.6, that uses f-strings and {} placeholders.

As you can see, while it is not possible to directly change or delete characters in a string, you can use various methods to create new strings with the desired modifications.

5.6.4 Python String Operations

In Python, there are several built-in operations that can be performed on strings, such as concatenation, repetition, and comparison.

String concatenation is the process of joining two or more strings together. This can be done using the + operator, or the join() method. String repetition is the process of repeating a string a certain number of times. This can be done using the * operator. String comparison is the process of comparing two strings to see if they are equal, or if one comes before the other in lexicographic order. This can be done using the ==, !=, >, <, >=, and <= operators.

Here is a single Python program that demonstrates some of these string operations:

```
# Concatenation
s1 = “Hello”
s2 = “World”
s3 = s1 + “, “ + s2 + “!”
print(s3) # “Hello, World!”

# Repetition
s4 = “Python “
s5 = s4 * 3
print(s5) # “Python Python Python “

# Comparison
s6 = “Python”
s7 = “python”
print(s6 == s7) # False
print(s6 != s7) # True
print(s6 > s7) # True
print(s6 < s7) # False

# Using join method
s8 = “ “.join([“Hello”,”World”])
print(s8) # “Hello World”
```

In the above program the first example shows the concatenation of two strings using + operator. The second example shows the repetition of a string using * operator. The third example shows the comparison of two strings using comparison operators like ==, !=, >, <, >=, and <=. The last example shows the use of join method to join multiple strings with a specified delimiter. You can use these string operations to perform various tasks such as formatting text, generating text output, and manipulating strings in your Python programs.

5.6.4.1 Concatenation

String concatenation is the process of joining two or more strings together to form a new string. In Python, there are several ways to concatenate strings, such as using the + operator, the += operator, the join() method or the f-strings.

Here is a single Python program that demonstrates some of these methods:

```
# Using the + operator
s1 = “Hello”
s2 = “World”
s3 = s1 + “ “ + s2
print(s3)  # “Hello World”

# Using the += operator
s4 = “Python”
s4 += “ is “
s4 += “powerful”
print(s4)  # “Python is powerful”

# Using the join() method
s5 = “ “.join([“Hello”,”World”])
print(s5) # “Hello World”

# Using f-strings
name = “John”
age = 30
s6 = f”My name is {name} and I am {age} years old”
print(s6) # “My name is John and I am 30 years old”
```

The first method uses the + operator to concatenate two strings. The second method uses the += operator to concatenate strings. The third method uses the join() method to join a list of strings with a specified delimiter. The last method uses f-strings, which were introduced in Python 3.6 and allow you to embed expressions inside string literals using {}.

5.6.4.2 Iteration and Membership Test

Iteration is the process of repeatedly executing a block of code for a given number of times or until a certain condition is met. In Python, this can be done using loops such as the for and while loops. Membership test is the process of checking if a specific element is present in a container object such as a list, tuple, set, or string. In Python, this can be done using the in and not in operators.

Here is a single Python program that demonstrates iteration and membership test using a string:

```
# Iteration using for loop
s = "Hello, World!"
for char in s:
    print(char)

# Iteration using while loop
i = 0
while i < len(s):
    print(s[i])
    i += 1

# Membership test using in and not in
s = "Hello, World!"
print("H" in s) # True
print("h" in s) # False
print("Z" not in s) # True
```

The first example uses a for loop to iterate over the characters of a string. The second example uses a while loop to iterate over the characters of a string, using the string's length to determine when to stop the loop. The last example uses the in and not in operators to check if a specific character is present in the string. The in operator returns True if the character is found in the string, False otherwise. The not in operator returns True if the character is not found in the string and False otherwise.

5.6.5 String Formatting

String formatting is the process of inserting values into a string. This can be done using string formatting methods such as format(), f-strings and string interpolation. These methods allow you to insert values into a string by defining placeholders in the string and then providing the values to be inserted.

Here is a single Python program that demonstrates different methods of string formatting:

```
# Using the format() method
name = "John"
age = 30
s = "My name is {} and I am {} years old".format(name, age)
print(s) # "My name is John and I am 30 years old"

# Using f-strings
name = "John"
age = 30
s = f"My name is {name} and I am {age} years old"
print(s) # "My name is John and I am 30 years old"

# Using string interpolation % operator
name = "John"
age = 30
s = "My name is %s and I am %d years old" % (name, age)
print(s) # "My name is John and I am 30 years old"
```

The first method uses the format() method to insert values into a string by defining placeholders in the string and then providing the values to be inserted. The second method uses f-strings, which were introduced in Python 3.6 and allow you to embed expressions inside string literals using {}. The last method uses the % operator to perform string interpolation in older version of python.

5.6.6 Python String Built-in Methods

In Python, strings have a variety of built-in methods that can be used to manipulate and interact with them. Some examples of these methods include:

- **upper():** Converts all characters in a string to uppercase
- **lower():** Converts all characters in a string to lowercase
- **replace(old, new):** Replaces all occurrences of the old substring with the new substring
- **find(sub):** Returns the index of the first occurrence of the substring
- **count(sub):** Returns the number of occurrences of the substring
- **split(sep):** Returns a list of substrings separated by the specified separator
- **strip():** Removes leading and trailing whitespace from a string
- **join(iterable):** Joins all elements in an iterable(list, tuple, etc) with the string as a separator

Here is a single Python program that demonstrates some of these methods:

```
s = “Hello, World!”

# Using upper() method
print(s.upper()) # “HELLO, WORLD!”

# Using lower() method
print(s.lower()) # “hello, world!”

# Using replace() method
print(s.replace(“World”, “Python”)) # “Hello, Python!”

# Using find() method
print(s.find(“World”)) # 7

# Using count() method
print(s.count(“o”)) # 2
```

```
# Using split() method
print(s.split(“,”)) # [“Hello”, “ World!”]

# Using strip() method
s = “  Hello, World!  “
print(s.strip()) # “Hello, World!”

# Using join() method
l = [“Hello”, “World”]
print(“, “.join(l)) # “Hello, World”
```

5.7 Summary

In this chapter, we covered the various native data types in Python in depth. These data types include numbers, strings, lists, tuples, sets, and dictionaries, and they provide different ways to store data in Python. We learned about the characteristics and uses of each data type, as well as the methods and functions associated with them. We also provided programming examples to illustrate the usage of each data type and its related methods and functions. Overall, this chapter aimed to give a comprehensive understanding of the different data types available in Python and how they can be used to store and manipulate data.

Review Questions

1. What are native data types in Python?
2. Can you explain the Python Number data type?
3. What is a List in Python and how is it used?
4. Can you describe the Python Tuple data type and its use?
5. How is a Set used in Python and what are its properties?
6. What is a Dictionary in Python and how is it different from a List or Tuple?
7. Can you give an example of how to create and use a Python String?
8. How are string operations, such as concatenation and slicing, performed in Python?

9. Can you explain the difference between single and double quotes in Python String definitions?
10. How can you format a Python String using the format() method?
11. Which of the following is a Python native data type that represents a sequence of characters?
    (a) Number
    (b) List
    (c) String
    (d) Dictionary
12. Which of the following is a Python native data type that represents an unordered collection of unique elements?
    (a) List
    (b) Tuple
    (c) Set
    (d) Dictionary

6

Python Functions

Highlights

- Python functions
- Types of functions
- Advantages of functions
- Python anonymous functions
- Pass by value vs. Pass by reference
- Recursion

Python functions are a fundamental concept in programming that allow you to encapsulate and reuse code. Functions in Python are blocks of code that perform a specific task and can be called multiple times throughout a program. They can take input parameters, return values, and modify global variables. Functions are defined using the "def" keyword, followed by a function name and any necessary parameters, and then the function body. To use a function, you simply call it by its name, passing any necessary arguments. Python functions can greatly simplify complex programs by breaking them down into smaller, reusable pieces of code.

6.1 Python Functions

In Python, a function is a block of code that performs a specific task and can be reused throughout your program. Functions are defined using the "def" keyword, followed by the function name and a set of parentheses for any input parameters. For example, you can define a function called "greet" that takes in a parameter called "name" and prints out a greeting message: "Hello, name!". Functions can also return a value using the "return" statement, for example, a function called "add" that takes in two parameters "a" and "b" and returns their sum. Functions are called by their name, followed by the parentheses and any necessary input arguments. Functions are useful for organizing and modularizing your code, making it easier to read, understand, and maintain. They also allow you to reuse the same code multiple times, without having to write it over and over again.

6.2 Advantages of Python

There are several advantages to using Python as a programming language:

1. **Easy to Learn and Read:** Python has a simple, easy-to-learn syntax which makes it a great language for beginners. It also uses indentation to indicate code blocks, making it more readable than other languages.
2. **Large and Active Community:** Python has a large and active community, which means that there are many resources available for learning and troubleshooting. Additionally, the community continually develops and maintains a wide range of libraries and frameworks, which makes development faster and more efficient.
3. **Versatile and Cross-Platform:** Python can be used for a wide range of tasks, including web development, scientific computing, data analysis, artificial intelligence, and more. It also runs on a variety of platforms, including Windows, Mac, and Linux.
4. **Plenty of Libraries and Frameworks:** Python has a wealth of libraries and frameworks available, including NumPy and SciPy for scientific computing, Pygame for game development, and Django and Flask for web development.
5. **Good for Prototyping:** Python's easy-to-read syntax and short development cycle make it a great choice for prototyping and experimenting with new ideas.
6. **High-Demand:** Python is one of the most popular programming languages, in demand by many industries, such as data science, machine learning, artificial intelligence, and web development.

6.3 Types of Functions

A function in Python is a block of reusable code that performs a specific task. Functions can accept input (referred to as arguments or parameters) and return output. Functions are defined using the def keyword, and are called using their name followed by parentheses, with any input passed within the parentheses.

There are two types of functions in Python:

1. Python User-defined Functions
2. Python Built-in Functions
3. Lambda Function
4. Recursive Function

1. **Built-in functions:** These are the functions that are already available in Python and can be used without importing any modules. Examples include print(), len(), and str().
2. **User-defined functions:** These are the functions that are defined by the user and can be reused throughout the program. These can take inputs and can return values.
3. **Anonymous or lambda functions:** These are the functions that are small and single-expression functions that are defined without a name, using the "lambda" keyword. These functions are useful for simple operations that can be defined in a single line of code.
4. **Recursive Function:** A function that calls itself is said to be recursive. In Python, recursion is a technique where a function calls itself in order to solve a problem.

6.4 Built-in Functions

Built-in functions are functions that are already available in Python and can be used without importing any modules. These functions are part of the Python standard library and are always available for use in your code. They can be used to perform a wide variety of tasks, such as converting data types, manipulating strings, and working with mathematical operations.Here's a table of some common built-in functions in Python:

Table 6.1 : Python Built in Functions

Function	Description
print()	Prints or displays text or data on the screen
input()	Gets input from the user
len()	Gets the length of a list, string, or other data structure
type()	Gets the data type of a variable or expression
int()	Converts a value to an integer
float()	Converts a value to a floating-point number
str()	Converts a value to a string
list()	Converts a value to a list
dict()	Converts a value to a dictionary
tuple()	Converts a value to a tuple

6.5 Python User Defined Functions

User-defined functions are functions that are created and defined by the user, as opposed to being built-in to the programming language or software system. These functions can be used to perform specific tasks or operations, and can be reused throughout a program or project.

Here's a table of some characteristics of user-defined functions in Python:

Table 6.2: Characteristics of user-defined function

Characteristics	Description
Definition	User-defined functions are defined using the def keyword, followed by the function name and a set of parentheses.
Parameters	User-defined functions can accept zero or more input parameters, which are specified within the parentheses.
Return value	User-defined functions can return zero or one value using the return keyword.
Scope	User-defined functions have their own scope and do not affect the global scope or other functions.
Reusability	User-defined functions can be called multiple times within a program or project, making the code more modular and reusable.
Naming	User-defined functions should be given a name that describes its functionality.

6.5.1 Function Definition

Function definition refers to the process of creating and specifying a function's code, its name, input parameters, and return value. In most programming languages, this is done using a specific syntax, such as the def keyword in Python. A user-defined function in Python is defined using the def keyword, followed by the function name, a set of parentheses (which may include input parameters), and a colon. The code that makes up the function's operations is then indented and placed beneath the definition.

```
Syntax:
def function_name():            //Definition of a function
        //Body of the function starts from here
```

For example:

```
def add_numbers(a,b):
        print("welcome!")
        return a+b
```

So body of the function is created.

6.5.2 Function Call

A function call is the process of invoking or executing a function. In other words, it's the process of telling the program to run the code inside a function. When a function is defined, it's created but not executed. It's only when the function is called that its code is executed. In order to call a function, you need to use the function's name followed by a set of parentheses, and inside these parentheses, you can pass any required parameters.

To call a function we simply type the function name with/without parameters as per functions definition..

```
Syntax:
def function_name():            //Definition of a function
        //Body of the function starts from here
function_name()         //Calling a function
```

Here's an example of a user-defined function in Python that takes two input parameters, a and b, and returns their sum:

Code 6.1: A program to add two numbers

```
def add_numbers(a, b):
    return a + b
result = add_numbers(3, 4)
print(result) # Output: 7
```

In this example, the function is named add_numbers and takes two input parameters a and b. The function's code is a single line that calculates the sum of a and b using the + operator and returns the result using the return keyword. When the function is called with the arguments 3 and 4, the return value is 7.

It's important to note that the same function can be called multiple times with different parameters, and it will execute its code each time, returning a different result based on the input values.

6.5.3 Types of Function Arguments(Parameters)

Function arguments, also known as parameters, are values that are passed to a function when it is called. These values are then used by the function to perform its designated task. In programming, there are several types of function arguments that can be used, each with their own specific characteristics and use cases. Understanding the different types of function arguments can help developers write more flexible and efficient code.

There are several types of function arguments (also known as parameters) in programming:

1. **Function with No Arguments:** A function with no arguments is a function that does not require any input values to be passed to it when it is called.
2. **Function with Required Arguments:** A function with required arguments is a function that requires specific input values to be passed to it when it is called. If these required arguments are not provided, the function will not be able to run or will raise an error.
3. **Function with Arbitrary Length Arguments:** A function with arbitrary length arguments is a function that can accept a variable number of input values. These values can be passed to the function using the *args or **kwargs notation.

4. **Function with Keyword Based Arguments:** A function with keyword-based arguments is a function that accepts input values that are passed to it by explicitly specifying the argument name and its value. This allows for more flexibility and readability in function calls.
5. **Function with Default Arguments:** A function with default arguments is a function that assigns default values to certain input parameters. If a value for these parameters is not provided when the function is called, the default value will be used.
6. **Python Anonymous Functions:** Anonymous functions are functions that are defined without a name. They are also known as lambda functions and can be used in situations where a function is required but a named function is not necessary. Anonymous functions can be defined using the lambda keyword in Python.

6.5.3.1 Function with No Arguments

A function with no arguments is a function that does not require any input values to be passed to it when it is called. Such functions can still perform useful operations, such as printing text, performing calculations, or returning a value. In Python, a function with no arguments can be defined using the def keyword, followed by the function name, a set of parentheses, and a colon. For example:

Code 6.2: Illustrate the function with no arguments.

```
def greet():
    print("Hello, World!")
greet() # Calling the function
```

In this example, the greet() function is defined using the def keyword, followed by the function name and a set of parentheses. There are no arguments defined within the parentheses, indicating that the function does not require any input values. The function simply prints a greeting message to the console when it is called. When the function is called by using the function name followed by parentheses, greet(), the function runs and prints "Hello, World!" as a output.

This example shows that a function with no arguments can still perform useful operations, such as printing a message or performing calculations.

6.5.3.2 Function with Required Arguments

A function with required arguments is a function that requires specific input values to be passed to it when it is called. These input values are defined as parameters within the function definition and are used by the function to perform its designated task. If these required arguments are not provided, the function will not be able to run or will raise an error. In Python, a function with required arguments can be defined using the def keyword, followed by the function name, a set of parentheses containing the required argument names, and a colon. For example:

Code 6.3: Illustrate the function with required arguments.

```
def greet(name):
    print(f'Hello, {name}!")
greet("John") # Calling the function with required argument
```

In this example, the greet() function is defined using the def keyword, followed by the function name and a set of parentheses containing one required argument named name. This argument is used to customize the greeting message that is printed to the console. When the function is called by using the function name followed by parentheses containing the required argument, greet("John"), the function runs and replaces the name placeholder in the greeting message with the provided value "John" , then it prints "Hello, John!" as a output.

```
Hello, John!
```

6.5.3.3 Function with Arbitrary Length Arguments

A function with arbitrary length arguments is a function that can accept a variable number of input values. These values can be passed to the function using the *args or **kwargs notation. In Python, *args allows a function to accept any number of positional arguments, while **kwargs allows a function to accept any number of keyword arguments. Here is an example of a function with arbitrary length arguments in Python:

Code 6.4:Illustrate the function with arbitrary length arguments.

```
def add_numbers(*numbers):
    result = 0
    for number in numbers:
        result += number
    return result
result = add_numbers(1,2,3,4,5)
print(result)
```

In this example, the add_numbers() function is defined using the def keyword, followed by the function name and a set of parentheses containing *numbers. The * before the argument name numbers indicates that the function can accept any number of positional arguments. The function then iterates over the numbers passed as arguments, adding them together and storing the result in a variable. Finally, the function returns the result. When the function is called by using the function name followed by parentheses containing the arbitrary length arguments, add_numbers(1,2,3,4,5), the function runs and adds all the numbers passed as arguments, then it prints 15 as a output.

It's also possible to use **kwargs to accept any number of keyword arguments, in this case the function would look like this:

```
def greet(**kwargs):
    print(f"Hello, {kwargs['name']}!")
greet(name="John")
```

In this example, the function is defined to accept any number of keyword arguments using **kwargs. The function then accesses the value of the "name" keyword argument and uses it to create a personalized greeting message.

6.5.3.4 Function with Keyword Based Arguments

A function with keyword-based arguments is a function that accepts input values that are passed to it by explicitly specifying the argument name and its value. This allows for more flexibility and readability in function calls, as it allows the developer to specify the arguments in any order, as well as to specify only the arguments that are relevant for the current call. In Python, keyword arguments are defined by including the argument name followed by an equal sign(=) and its value in the function call. Here is an example of a function with keyword-based arguments in Python:

Code 6.5: Illustrate the function with keyword arguments.

```
def greet(name, age):
    print(f"Hello, {name}. You are {age} years old.")
greet(age=25, name="John")
```

In this example, the greet() function is defined using the def keyword, followed by the function name and a set of parentheses containing two arguments name and age.

When the function is called by using the function name followed by parentheses containing the keyword-based arguments, greet(age=25, name="John"), the function runs and replaces the name and age placeholders in the greeting message with the provided values "John" and 25, respectively, then it prints "Hello, John. You are 25 years old." as a output.

It's also possible to specify some of the arguments as keyword arguments and others as positional arguments, for example:

```
greet("John", age=25)
```

This will also run the same way and prints the same output as before.

6.5.3.5 Function with Default Arguments

A function with default arguments is a function that assigns default values to certain input parameters. If a value for these parameters is not provided when the function is called, the default value will be used. In Python, default arguments are defined by including the argument name followed by an equal sign(=) and its default value in the function definition.

Here is an example of a function with default arguments in Python:

Code 6.6: Illustrate the function with default arguments.

```
def greet(name, age=25):
    print(f"Hello, {name}. You are {age} years old.")
greet("John")
```

In this example, the greet() function is defined using the def keyword, followed by the function name and a set of parentheses containing two arguments name and age. The age argument has a default value of 25. When the function is called by using the function name followed by parentheses containing the only required argument, greet("John"), the function runs and uses the default value of 25 for the age argument, then it prints "Hello, John. You are 25 years old." as a output.

6.6 Python Anonymous Functions

In Python, anonymous functions are functions that are defined without a name. They are also known as lambda functions and can be used in situations where a function is required but a named function is not necessary. Anonymous functions can be defined using the lambda keyword in Python.

```
Syntax:
lambda arguments: expression
```

The lambda keyword is used to define an anonymous functions in Python. Usually, such a function is meant for one-time use.

This function can have any number of arguments but only one expression, which is evaluated and returned. One is free to use lambda functions wherever function objects are required.

Here is an example of an anonymous function in Python:

Code 6.7 : Illustrate the use of lambda function

```
x = lambda a : a + 10
print(x(5))
```

In this example, the anonymous function is defined using the lambda keyword, followed by the argument(s) and the function's expression. The function takes one argument a and returns the value of a plus 10. When the function is called by providing the argument 5 as input, x(5), the function runs and returns the value 5+10=15 as output.

Here is an example of an anonymous function with multiple arguments:

```
x = lambda a,b,c : a + b + c
print(x(2,5,8))
```

Lambda functions are commonly used when a small, one-time-use function is required. They can also be used as a function argument, for example, as a sorting key function, a filter function, a map function, and so on. It's also possible to use lambda functions in combination with other built-in functions such as map, filter, and reduce.

```
numbers = [1, 2, 3, 4, 5]
squared_numbers = map(lambda x: x**2, numbers)
print(list(squared_numbers)) # Output: [1, 4, 9, 16, 25]
```

6.6.1 Characteristics of Lambda Form

A lambda form, also known as a lambda function, is a way to create small, anonymous functions in Python. These functions are defined using the "lambda" keyword, followed by a list of arguments, a colon, and the function's expression. Here is an example of a simple lambda form that takes in one argument (x) and returns its square:

```
square = lambda x: x*x
```

The main characteristics of lambda forms are:

1. **Anonymous:** Lambda forms do not have a name, and they cannot be referenced by name.
2. **Small:** Lambda forms are usually only one line of code, and they are typically used for simple operations.
3. **Function objects:** Lambda forms can be used wherever a function object is required, such as being passed as an argument to another function.
4. **Assignable:** Lambda forms can be assigned to a variable, allowing them to be passed as an argument or returned from a function.
5. **Functional programming:** Lambda forms can be used with the map(), filter() and reduce() functions for functional programming.
6. **Single expression:** Lambda forms are limited to a single expression, unlike regular functions which can have multiple statements.
7. **No return statement:** Lambda forms do not have a return statement, and whatever is after the colon is returned.

Please note that, while lambda forms are useful in certain cases, they should be used with caution. They can make code harder to read and understand, especially if they are used extensively or in complex ways.

6.7 Pass by Value vs. Pass by Reference

In Python, all variables are passed by reference. This means that when a variable is passed as an argument to a function, the function receives the memory address of the variable, not a copy of its value. Any changes made to the variable within the function will affect the original variable. For example, if you pass a list to a function and modify the list within the function, the original list will be modified as well.

However, when a primitive value such as an integer or string is passed to a function, the function receives a reference to the object containing the value rather than the value itself. This means that the function can change the attributes of the object, but the value of the primitive can not be changed. For example, if you pass an integer toInside the function, x is: 11

Outside the function, x is: 10

a function and change the value of the integer within the function, the original integer will not be changed.

6.7.1 Pass by Value

In Python, all variables are passed by reference, which means that when a variable is passed as an argument to a function, the function receives the memory address of the variable, not a copy of its value. Any changes made to the variable within the function will affect the original variable. However, when a primitive value such as an integer or string is passed to a function, the function receives a reference to the object containing the value rather than the value itself. This means that the function can change the attributes of the object, but the value of the primitive can not be changed.

Here is an example of passing an integer by reference in Python:

```
def increment(x):
    x += 1
    print("Inside the function, x is:", x)
x = 10
increment(x)
print("Outside the function, x is:", x)
```

This program will output:

```
Inside the function, x is: 11
Outside the function, x is: 10
```

As you can see, the function modifies the value of the variable x within the function, but this change does not affect the original variable x outside the function. This is because the variable x is passed by reference, but the value of x can not be modified.

6.7.2 Pass by Object Reference

In Python, all variables are passed by object reference, which means that when a variable is passed as an argument to a function, the function receives the memory address of the object, not a copy of its value. Any changes made to the object within the function will affect the original object. For example, if you pass a list to a function and modify the list within the function, the original list will be modified as well.

Here is an example of passing a list by object reference in Python:

```
def increment(lst):
    lst[0] += 1
    print("Inside the function, the list is:", lst)
lst = [10, 20, 30]
increment(lst)
print("Outside the function, the list is:", lst)
```

This program will output:

```
Inside the function, the list is: [11, 20, 30]
Outside the function, the list is: [11, 20, 30]
```

As you can see, the function modifies the value of the first element of the list lst within the function, and this change affects the original list lst outside the function as well. This is because the list lst is passed by object reference, and the object can be modified.

It's also worth noting that in python, some types are mutable and some are immutable, for example, lists are mutable and tuples are immutable.

6.8 Recursion

In computer science, recursion is a method of solving a problem by breaking it down into smaller, identical problems. A function that calls itself is said to be recursive. In Python, recursion is a technique where a function calls itself in order to solve a problem.

Recursion is a powerful problem-solving technique that can be used to solve many types of problems, such as mathematical problems, tree traversals, and more. The key to using recursion effectively is to find the base case, which is the simplest version of the problem that can be solved directly, and the recursive case, which is the problem broken down into smaller identical parts.

Here's an example of a simple recursive function in Python:

Code 6.8: Illustrator the concept of recursion in python.

```
def factorial(n):
    if n == 0:
        return 1
    else:
        return n * factorial(n-1)
print(factorial(5)) # 120
```

This function calculates the factorial of a number. The base case is when n is 0, and the function returns 1. In the recursive case, the function calls itself with the argument n-1, which is a smaller version of the problem. The function will continue to call itself with smaller and smaller arguments until the base case is reached and the function can return a value.

Recursion can be a powerful and elegant way to solve problems, but it can also be hard to understand, and it can consume a lot of memory if not used carefully, as each call creates a new call stack frame, and if the recursion depth is large it can cause a stack overflow error.

6.8.1 Advantages of Recursion

Recursion is a powerful problem-solving technique that can be used to solve many types of problems in Python, and it has several advantages:

1. **Clarity and Simplicity:** Recursive solutions can be simple and easy to understand, especially for problems that have a natural recursive structure.
2. **Conciseness:** Recursive solutions can be more concise than their iterative counterparts, as they eliminate the need for explicit looping and counter variables.
3. **Reusability:** Recursive functions can be reused for solving similar problems with different inputs, making the code more modular and easy to maintain.
4. **Elegance:** Recursive solutions can be elegant and visually pleasing, as they capture the natural structure of the problem and express it in a clear and concise way.
5. **Flexibility:** Recursive solutions can be adapted and extended to solve more complex problems, as they can be combined with other techniques, such as dynamic programming and memoization, to optimize their performance.

It's worth noting that recursion has also some drawbacks, like consuming a lot of memory and the risk of stack overflow errors, and it might not always be the best solution for a given problem, it's important to consider the complexity and performance of the algorithm before choosing recursion as the solution.

6.8.2 Disadvantages of Recursion

Recursion is a programming technique where a function calls itself in order to solve a problem. This technique is used to solve problems that can be broken down into smaller, similar problems. In Python, recursion is implemented using function calls.

Disadvantages of recursion in python are:

1. It can be more difficult to understand and debug compared to iterative solutions.
2. It can consume a large amount of memory due to the call stack.
3. The risk of stack overflow error if the recursion goes too deep.
4. It can be less efficient as compared to iterative solution due to the overhead of function calls.
5. Recursive solutions may be less readable and harder to maintain than their iterative counterparts.
6. A problem that can be solved using a loop may use unnecessary additional function calls with recursion.
7. Recursive solutions may not always be the best choice for solving a problem and may result in slower performance.

6.9 Scope and Lifetime of Variables

In Python, a variable's scope refers to the portion of the program where the variable can be accessed. The lifetime of a variable refers to the period of time that a variable exists and retains its value.

There are two types of scope in Python:

1. **Local scope**: A variable defined within a function or a block of code has a local scope and can only be accessed within that function or block.
2. **Global scope:** A variable defined outside of any function or block has a global scope and can be accessed throughout the entire program.

The lifetime of a variable in Python depends on where the variable is defined:

Variables defined within a function have a lifetime that lasts only as long as the function call. Once the function call is finished, the variable is destroyed.

Variables defined outside of any function have a lifetime that lasts as long as the program is running. Once the program exits, the variable is destroyed.

It's important to note that in python, you can use global keyword inside function to make a variable global, otherwise it will be treated as local variable

6.10 Summary

In this chapter, we explored the concept of functions in the Python programming language. We covered both built-in functions and user-defined functions, providing a comprehensive list of built-in functions and detailing the various types of user-defined functions with examples. We also delved into the topic of anonymous functions, which are created using the lambda function, and discussed the concepts of pass by value and pass by object reference. Additionally, we covered the topic of recursion, which is a powerful tool for solving certain types of problems. Finally, we discussed the scope and lifetime of variables and how they relate to functions.

Review Questions

1. What is a function in Python?
2. How do you define a function in Python?
3. What is the difference between a built-in function and a user-defined function in Python?
4. What is a return statement in Python functions and why is it important?
5. What is the scope of a variable defined inside a function in Python?
6. What is a default argument in Python functions and how is it used?
7. What is a lambda function in Python?
8. What is recursion in Python and how is it implemented?
9. What is a function decorator in Python?
10. How can you pass a function as an argument to another function in Python?

11. Which of the following is not a type of function in Python?
    (a) Built-in functions
    (b) User-defined functions
    (c) Anonymous functions
    (d) Binary functions
12. Which of the following describes how Python passes arguments to a function?
    (a) Pass by value
    (b) Pass by reference
    (c) Pass by object reference
    (d) Pass by copy

7

Python Modules

Highlights

- Python Modules
- Creating a Module
- Importing Module
- Standard Modules
- Python Packages

A module in Python is a file containing Python definitions and statements. The file name is the module name with the suffix .py added. Modules can define functions, classes, and variables, and can also include runnable code. The import statement is used to include a module in a Python script and access the definitions and statements defined within the module. Additionally, specific functions or variables can be imported from a module using the from ... import ... statement. Aliases can also be assigned to modules or functions using the as keyword when importing.

Modules can also be included in Python's built-in library, such as sys and os, which provide access to certain variables and functions used or maintained by the interpreter and operating system functionality respectively.

7.1 Need of Module

Modules are a fundamental concept in programming and are used to organize and reuse code. They are a way to divide a large program into smaller and more manageable parts. By breaking code into modules, you can make it easier to understand, maintain, and update. Modules provide a way to organize related code and variables into a separate namespace, which helps to avoid naming conflicts and makes your code more organized and readable. Additionally, modules allow you to reuse code across multiple projects, saving time and effort. Modules also make it easy to use the built-in and third-party functionality in Python. Python has a large library of built-in modules that provide a wide range of functionality, and a large community of developers who have created a wide variety of modules that can be imported and used in your code. This makes it easy to accomplish certain tasks, such as machine learning, web scraping, and more.

Modules in Python serve several purposes, including:

1. **Code Reusability:** Modules allow you to organize your code into reusable and self-contained blocks. This means that you can write a module once and use it in multiple projects, saving time and effort.
2. **Namespace:** Modules provide a way to organize related code and variables into a separate namespace. This helps to avoid naming conflicts and makes your code more organized and readable.
3. **Code Maintenance:** Modules help to separate different parts of your code and make it easier to maintain. You can make changes to a module without having to worry about affecting other parts of your code.
4. **Standard Library:** Python has a large library of built-in modules that provide a wide range of functionality, including file handling, string manipulation, mathematical functions, and more. These modules can be imported and used in your code, saving time and effort in developing your own solutions.
5. **Third-party Libraries:** Python has a large community of developers who have created a wide variety of modules that can be imported and used in your code. These libraries provide additional functionality and can make it easier to accomplish certain tasks, such as machine learning, web scraping, and more.

In summary, modules help you to organize your code, increase code reusability, and make it easy to use the built-in and third-party functionality.

7.2 Module Definition

A module in Python is a file containing Python definitions and statements. The file name is the module name with the suffix .py added. For example, a file named "example.py" would be considered a module in Python. A module can contain various types of definitions such as functions, classes, and variables, and can also include runnable code. Functions and classes defined in a module can be called and instantiated by other parts of the program. Variables defined in a module can be accessed and modified by other parts of the program.

You can create a module by creating a new .py file and adding your Python code to it. Once the module is created, it can be imported into other Python scripts using the import statement and the definitions and statements within the module can be accessed using the dot notation. For example, if you have a module called example.py that defines a function called example_function, you can import the module and call the function like this:

```
import example
example.example_function()
```

It's worth noting that, python also have a mechanism of package which is a collection of related modules. With packages, you can organize your modules into a single namespace, making it easy to keep related modules together and organized.

7.3 Creating a Module

Creating a module in Python is as simple as creating a new .py file and adding your Python code to it. Here are the basic steps to create a module:

1. Open a text editor or an IDE, such as IDLE or PyCharm.
2. Create a new file and save it with a .py file extension. The name of the file will be the name of the module. For example, if you want to create a module called "example", you would save the file as "example.py".
3. Add your Python code to the file. You can define functions, classes, and variables in the module. For example:

   Code 7.1: Illustrating the concept of module in python

   ```
   def example_function():
       print("This is an example function.")
   ```

```
class ExampleClass:
    pass
example_variable = "This is an example variable."
```

4. Save the file.

   To use the module in another Python script, you need to import it using the import statement. For example:

```
import example
example.example_function()
```

   Once the module is imported, you can access the functions, classes and variables that are defined inside that module, using the dot notation. It's also worth noting that, if you want to make some of the functions, classes or variables defined in the module to be accessible by importing the module directly, you can use the __all__ variable in the module.

```
__all__ = ["example_function", "ExampleClass"]
```

This will make only the example_function and ExampleClass available when importing the module directly.

7.4 Importing Module in the Interpreter

In Python, you can import a module using the "import" keyword. For example, to import the "math" module, you would use the following command:

```
import math
```

Once the module is imported, you can access its functions and variables using the dot notation. For example, you can use the "math.sqrt()" function to find the square root of a number.

Code 7.2: A program to find the square root of a number.

```
import math
print(math.sqrt(16)) # Output: 4.0
```

You can also use the "from" keyword to import specific functions or variables from a module. For example, to import only the "sqrt" function from the "math" module, you would use the following command:

```
from math import sqrt
print(sqrt(16)) # Output: 4.0
```

You can also use the "as" keyword to give a module a different name when importing it. For example, to import the "math" module as "m", you would use the following command:

```
import math as m
print(m.sqrt(16)) # Output: 4.0
```

7.5 Importing Module in the Another Script

To import a module in another script in Python, use the import statement followed by the name of the module you wish to import. For example, if you want to import the math module, you would use the following statement:

```
import math
```

Once the module is imported, you can use its functions and variables by referencing them with the module name as a prefix. For example, you can use the math.sqrt() function to calculate the square root of a number.

```
import math
x = math.sqrt(16)
print(x)
```

You can also import specific functions or variables from a module using the from keyword, followed by the name of the module, and then the name of the function or variable you wish to import. For example:

Code 7.3: Illustrate the use of from keyword to import a module.

```
from math import sqrt
x = sqrt(16)
print(x)
```

This can be useful if you only need to use a small number of functions or variables from a module and do not want to have to use the module name as a prefix every time you use them.

7.6 Importing Modules

In Python, modules are libraries of pre-written code that you can use in your own programs. To use a module in a Python script, you need to import it using the import statement.

We can load module in python using two ways:

- **The import statement**
- **The from-import statement**

For example, to import the math module, you would use the following command:

```
import math
```

This makes all of the functions and variables defined in the math module available for use in your script. Once a module is imported, you can call its functions by prefixing the function name with the name of the module. For example:

```
import math
x = math.sqrt(16)
print(x)
```

This would output the square root of 16, which is 4.0.

You can also import specific variables or functions from a module using the from keyword. For example, to import only the sqrt function from the math module, you would use the following command:

```
from math import sqrt
x = sqrt(16)
print(x)
```

This would also output 4.0.

7.7 Search Path of Module

In Python, when you import a module, the interpreter searches for it in a list of directories called the "module search path." The search path is stored in the sys.path variable, which is a list of strings. By default, the search path includes the directory containing the script being run, as well as several standard library directories and the site-packages directory of the current Python installation.

You can see the current module search path by importing the sys module and printing the value of sys.path. For example:

Code:7.5 : Illustrate the concept of serach path by importing the sys module.

```
import sys
print(sys.path)
```

You can also add new directories to the module search path by modifying the sys.path variable. For example, to add a directory called my_modules to the search path, you would use the following command:

```
import sys
sys.path.append("my_modules")
```

This would allow you to import modules from the my_modules directory as if they were part of the standard library. It's also worth noting that you can use PYTHONPATH environment variable to specify additional directories to be searched for modules.

It's important to keep in mind that modifying the module search path can make your code less portable, as the modules you import may not be available on other systems or in other environments.

7.8 Module Reloading

In Python, when you import a module, the interpreter caches the module's code in memory. This means that if you make changes to the module's code and then re-import it, the changes will not be reflected in your script unless you explicitly reload the module. You can reload a module using the importlib. reload() function, which is part of the importlib module. This function takes a single argument, which is the module you want to reload. For example, to reload the math module, you would use the following command:

Code:7.6 : Illustrate the concept of reloading a module in python.

```
import importlib
importlib.reload(math)
```

It's important to note that reload() function only available in python3.4 and above. In python 2, you can use reload() function from imp module.

```
from imp import reload
reload(math)
```

It's worth noting that reloading a module can cause problems if the module's code has changed in such a way that it is no longer compatible with the code that is using it. It's always a good idea to test your code thoroughly after reloading a module to make sure that everything is still working as expected.

Additionally, it's not necessary to reload a module when you are developing and testing your code. Python interpreter automatically reloads the module when you run the code again.

7.9 The dir() Function

The dir() function in Python is used to find out the names of all attributes and methods associated with an object. It takes an object as its argument and returns a list of strings that contain the names of the attributes and methods of the object. For example, if you call dir(str), it will return a list of all the attributes and methods that can be used with strings. If you call dir() without any arguments, it returns a list of names in the current local scope or global scope.

The syntax of the dir() function is as follows:

```
dir([object])
```

Where object is an optional argument that specifies the object whose attributes and methods you want to display. If no argument is passed, dir() will display the names in the current local or global scope.

Here is an example of using dir() to display the attributes and methods of a list object:

```
>>> my_list = [1, 2, 3]
>>> dir(my_list)
['__add__', '__class__', '__contains__', '__delattr__', '__delitem__', '__dir__', '__doc__', '__eq__', '__format__', '__ge__', '__getattribute__', '__getitem__', '__gt__', '__hash__', '__iadd__', '__imul__', '__init__', '__init_subclass__', '__iter__', '__le__', '__len__', '__lt__', '__mul__', '__ne__', '__new__', '__reduce__', '__reduce_ex__', '__repr__', '__reversed__', '__rmul__', '__setattr__', '__setitem__', '__sizeof__', '__str__', '__subclasshook__', 'append', 'clear', 'copy', 'count', 'extend', 'index', 'insert', 'pop', 'remove', 'reverse', 'sort']
```

7.10 Standard Modules

The Python Standard Library is a collection of modules that are included with the Python programming language. These modules provide a wide range of functionality and are designed to be easy to use and efficient. They are written in Python and are available for use in any Python program, without the need for additional installation. The Standard Library is organized into several sub-categories, such as built-in functions, data types, files and directories, internet and protocols, and many more.

Here is a table that provides a brief introduction to some of the most commonly used standard modules in Python:

Table 7.1: Standard modules in Python

Module	Descriptionjson
os	Provides a way to interact with the operating system and perform tasks such as navigating the file system, manipulating files and directories, and interacting with environment variables.
sys	Provides access to interpreter-specific functions and variables, such as the command-line arguments, the interpreter's version and build information, and the current working directory.
math	Provides mathematical functions and constants, such as trigonometric functions, logarithmic functions, and the mathematical constant pi.
random	Provides functions to generate pseudo-random numbers and perform random sampling from different distributions.
time	Provides functions to handle time, including the ability to get the current time, sleep, and convert between different time representations.
re	Provides regular expression matching operations, including functions to search for patterns in strings, split strings based on a pattern, and replace text based on a pattern.
json	Provides functions to encode and decode JSON data.
datetime	Provides classes for working with dates and times, including the ability to perform arithmetic with dates and times, and format dates and times as strings.
urllib	Provides functions to open URLs, including functions to retrieve data from the web, send data to the web, and handle cookies.
collections	Provides alternatives to built-in types that can be more efficient in certain cases, such as ordered dictionaries and defaultdicts.

There are many more modules available in the Standard Library, and you can find more information about them in the Python documentation.

7.11 Python Packages

Python packages are collections of modules that provide additional functionality to the Python programming language. These modules can be imported into a Python script and used to perform specific tasks. Some popular Python packages include NumPy for scientific computing, Pandas for data manipulation, and Matplotlib for data visualization.

To use a package in your Python script, you first need to install it. The most common way to install a package is using pip, which is a package manager for Python. To install a package using pip, you can use the following command:

```
pip install package_name
```

Once a package is installed, you can import it into your script using the import statement. Here's an example of importing the NumPy package:

```
import numpy as np
```

In the above example numpy is the package name and np is the alias which we are giving to the package so that we don't have to write numpy everytime, instead we can use np.

Once a package is imported, you can use its functions and methods to perform various tasks. Here's an example of using the NumPy package to create an array:

Code: 7.7: Code:7.5 : Illustrate the concept of packages in python.

```
import numpy as np
# Create a 1-dimensional array
a = np.array([1, 2, 3, 4, 5])
# Print the array
print(a)
```

This will create an array with the values 1, 2, 3, 4, and 5, and print it out.

You can also import specific modules or functions from a package using the from statement, like this:

```
from numpy import array
a = array([1, 2, 3, 4, 5])
```

It is also possible to import multiple packages in a single import statement:

```
import numpy as np, pandas as pd
```

7.12 Summary

In this chapter, we covered the topic of creating modules, which are a type of user-defined function that can be reused across multiple scripts. We went over the concept of modules, how they are defined and created, and provided examples of how to import them in both interpreter and script mode. Additionally, we discussed the process of finding modules using the search path and the dir() function. We also touched on the topic of built-in standard modules and concluded with information on creating and utilizing packages.

Review Questions

1. What is a module in Python?
2. How do you create a module in Python?
3. What is the syntax for importing a module in Python?
4. What is the difference between the import and from...import statements in Python?
5. How can you access functions defined in a module in Python?
6. What is the purpose of a name variable in a Python module?
7. What are standard modules in Python and how are they useful?
8. What is a package in Python?
9. How do you create a package in Python?
10. What is the difference between a module and a package in Python?
11. Which of the following statements is true about importing modules in Python?
    (a) You can only import one module at a time using the import statement
    (b) You can import multiple modules at once using the from...import statement
    (c) You can import a module and its functions using the as keyword
    (d) You can only import built-in modules in Python
12. Which of the following is not a standard module in Python?
    (a) os
    (b) sys
    (c) random
    (d) mathplotlib

8

Exception Handling

Highlights

- Python Exception
- Python Built-in Exceptions
- Exception Handling
- Python User-Defined Exceptions

An exception in Python is an event that occurs during the execution of a program that disrupts the normal flow of instructions. When an exception occurs, the program will stop running and an exception object will be created, containing information about the error. This allows the program to handle the exception and take appropriate action, such as displaying an error message or attempting to recover from the error. Exceptions can be raised explicitly using the "raise" statement, or they can be raised implicitly by the Python interpreter when an error occurs. It is also possible to handle exceptions using try-except blocks, which allows the program to catch and handle specific exceptions while allowing others to continue propagating.

8.1 Exception

In Python, an exception is an event that occurs during the execution of a program that disrupts the normal flow of instructions. Exceptions are typically caused by errors in the program, such as division by zero, accessing an index out of range, or a file not found. When an exception occurs, the program will stop running and an exception object will be created, containing information about the error. It allows the program to handle the exception and take appropriate action, such as displaying an error message or attempting to recover from the error. The Python interpreter has a set of built-in exceptions that can be raised, and it is also possible for the user to define their own exception classes.

8.2 Python Built-in Exceptions

Python has a set of built-in exceptions that are raised when certain errors occur during the execution of a program. These exceptions are defined in the built-in "exceptions" module and are derived from the base class "BaseException".

Here is a list of some common built-in exceptions in Python:

Table 8.1 : Built in exceptions in python

Exception	Cause
AssertionError	Raised when an assert statement fails.
AttributeError	Raised when an attribute reference or assignment fails.
EOFError	Raised when the input() function hits an end-of-file condition (EOF) without reading any data.
FileNotFoundError	Raised when a file or directory is requested but doesn't exist.
FloatingPointError	Raised when a floating point operation fails.
ImportError	Raised when an import statement fails to find the module definition or when a from...import statement fails to find a name that is to be imported.
IndexError	Raised when an index is not found in a sequence.
KeyError	Raised when a key is not found in a dictionary.
NameError	Raised when a variable is not found in the local or global namespace.
TypeError	Raised when an operation or function is applied to an object of an inappropriate type.
ValueError	Raised when a built-in operation or function receives an argument that has the right type but an inappropriate value.
ZeroDivisionError	Raised when the second operand of a division or modulo operation is zero.

8.3 Exception Handling

Before we understand the exception handling let we shed some light on what Exception is.

When a python program terminates as soon as it encounters an error. In Python, an error can be a syntax error or an exception. Hence, the exceptions should be properly handled so that an abrupt termination of the program is prevented.

Exception handling in Python is a mechanism for handling errors and exceptional conditions in your code. It allows you to write code that can gracefully handle unexpected conditions, such as a missing file or a network connection error, without causing the entire program to crash. In Python, exceptions are raised when something unexpected or exceptional occurs in the program, such as a divide-by-zero error or an attempt to access a non-existent element in a list. When an exception is raised, the normal flow of control in the program is interrupted, and the program looks for a piece of code that can handle the exception.

Process of Exception Handling involves following important terms:

- **try** : try block used to keep the block of code that may raise e
- **except** : to handle the exception after catching it.
- **else** : it runs when no exception exist
- **finally** : finally block will always execute no matter what

To handle exceptions in Python, you use the try and except statements. The try block contains the code that may raise an exception, and the except block contains the code that will be executed if an exception is raised. For example:

Code 8.1: Illustrate the use of try and except.

```
try:
    x = 1 / 0
except ZeroDivisionError:
    print("Cannot divide by zero.")
```

In this example, the try block contains a division operation that may raise a ZeroDivisionError exception, and the except block contains a message that will be printed if the exception is raised.

You can also use the finally block which contains code that will be executed regardless of whether an exception was raised or not. And else block which will be executed if no exception is raised in the try block.

It's also possible to use raise statement to raise an exception.

```
if x < 0:
    raise ValueError("x should be positive.")
```

8.3.1 Try, Except, Else and Finally

In Python, the try, except, and finally statements are used for exception handling.

The **try** block contains the code that may raise an exception. If an exception is raised, the normal flow of control in the program is interrupted, and the program looks for an except block that can handle the exception.

The **except** block contains the code that will be executed if an exception is raised in the corresponding try block. It can handle specific exceptions, like:

```
try:
    x = 1 / 0
except ZeroDivisionError:
    print("Cannot divide by zero.")
```

You can also handle multiple exceptions by using multiple except blocks.If the type of exception doesn't match any of the except blocks, it will remain unhandled and the program will terminate.

For example:

```
try:
        x=10
        y=0
        print (x/y)
except TypeError:
        print('Unsupported operation')
except ZeroDivisionError:
        print ('Cannot divide by zero')
```

Result:

Cannot divide by zero

The **else block** contain the code that will execute when there is no exception in try block. The except block is executed if the exception occurs inside the try block, otherwise the else block gets processed if the try block is found to be exception free.

Code 8.2: Illustrate the use of try except and else.

```
try:
            x=20
            y=10
    z= x/y
        print (z)
except ZeroDivisionError:
    print ('Cannot divide by zero')
else:
    print('The result of division of x and y is',z)
```

Output:

2.0

The result of division of x and y is 2.0

The **finally** block contains code that will be executed regardless of whether an exception was raised or not. The code in this block is guaranteed to be executed, even if an exception is raised in the try block or not.

Code 8.3: A program to demonstrate the use of finally keyword.

```
try:
  x = 1 / 0
except ZeroDivisionError:
  print("Cannot divide by zero.")
finally:
  print("This block will always be executed.")
```

It's often used to release resources like file handlers, network connections, etc.

In summary, the try block contains the code that may raise an exception, the except block contains the code that will be executed if an exception is raised and the finally block contains code that will always be executed regardless of whether an exception was raised or not.

8.3.2 Catching Specific Exceptions in Python

In Python, you can catch specific exceptions by using the except statement along with the specific exception you want to catch. For example:

```
try:
    x = 1 / 0
except ZeroDivisionError:
    print("Cannot divide by zero.")
```

In this example, the try block contains a division operation that may raise a ZeroDivisionError exception, and the except block contains a message that will be printed if the exception is raised.

You can also catch multiple specific exceptions in a single except block by providing a tuple of exception types.

```
try:
    x = int("hello")
except (ValueError, TypeError):
    print("Invalid input.")
```

In this example, the try block contains a conversion operation that may raise a ValueError or TypeError exception, and the except block contains a message that will be printed if either of those exceptions is raised. You can also use the as keyword to assign the raised exception to a variable.

```
try:
    x = 1 / 0
except ZeroDivisionError as e:
    print("Cannot divide by zero. Reason: ", e)
```

In this example, the ZeroDivisionError exception is caught and assigned to the variable e, which can be used to access the exception's information. It's also a good practice to catch the most specific exception first, and then catch more general exceptions. This is because if you catch a general exception first, it will catch all the exceptions including the specific one, thus not giving a chance for the specific exception to be handled.

8.3.3 try....finally

In Python, the try and finally statements are used to handle exceptions (i.e. run-time errors) in a controlled way. The try block contains the code that may raise an exception, and the finally block contains code that will always be executed, whether an exception is raised or not.

Here's an example of how to use the try and finally statements in a program:

```
try:
    # code that may raise an exception
    x = 1 / 0
except ZeroDivisionError:
    # code to handle the exception
    print("Cannot divide by zero!")
finally:
    # code that will always be executed
    print("The 'try' block has finished executing.")
```

In the above code, the try block contains the code x = 1 / 0, which raises a ZeroDivisionError exception because it is attempting to divide by zero. The except block then catches the exception and prints a message to the user. The finally block then runs and prints another message, indicating that the try block has finished executing. It is important to note that the finally block will always be executed, even if there is a return statement or an unhandled exception in the try block.

8.4 Python User Defined Exceptions

In Python, you can define your own custom exceptions by creating a new class that inherits from the built-in Exception class. This allows you to create specific types of exceptions that are tailored to the needs of your program.

Here's an example of how to create a custom exception class:

Code 8.4: Illustrating the use of raise keyword in user defined exception.

```
class CustomException(Exception):
    def __init__(self, message):
        self.message = message
raise CustomException("This is a custom exception.")
```

In the above code, we create a new class called CustomException that inherits from the built-in Exception class. We also define an __init__ method that takes a message as an argument, which allows us to specify a custom error message when we raise the exception.

Here's an example of how you might use the custom exception in a program:

Code 8.5: A program to validate the age.

```
class InvalidAgeError(Exception):
    pass


def validate_age(age):
    if age < 0:
        raise InvalidAgeError("Age cannot be negative.")
    elif age > 150:
        raise InvalidAgeError("Age cannot be greater than 150.")
    else:
        print("Age is valid.")


try:
    validate_age(-5)
except InvalidAgeError as e:
    print(e)
```

In this example, we define a function validate_age that raises an InvalidAgeError exception if the age passed to it is less than 0 or greater than 150. We then call the function in a try block and catch the exception if it is raised, printing the error message.

8.5 Summary

In this chapter, we covered the topics of interpreting time errors (syntax errors) and run-time errors, also known as exceptions. Python has a variety of built-in exceptions that can be used to handle different situations that may arise during the execution of a program. Additionally, users have the capability to create their own custom exceptions to handle specific circumstances. We discussed the use of the try, except, and finally constructs, providing examples to illustrate their use. Furthermore, we explained how to create user-defined exceptions and provided an example to demonstrate its usage.

Review Questions

1. What is an exception in Python?
2. How do you handle exceptions in Python?
3. What is the purpose of the try...except statement in Python?
4. What is the syntax for raising an exception in Python?
5. What is a built-in exception in Python and how is it used?
6. What is the difference between an error and an exception in Python?
7. What is a traceback in Python and how can it be used?
8. What is a user-defined exception in Python and how is it created?
8. What is the purpose of the finally clause in a try...except statement in Python?
9. What is the purpose of the assert statement in Python?
10. Which of the following is not a built-in exception in Python?
    (a) ZeroDivisionError
    (b) IndexError
    (c) UserWarning
    (d) ImportError
11. Which of the following is true about exception handling in Python?
    (a) The try...except statement can qhandle any type of exception
    (b) The finally clause is optional in a try...except statement
    (c) User-defined exceptions cannot be raised in Python
    (d) The raise statement is used to handle exceptions in Python

9

File Management in Python

Highlights

- Operations on Files
- write() and read() Methods
- Python File Methods
- Renaming and Deleting Files
- Directories in Python

Python provides several ways to work with files, including the built-in open() function, which allows you to read, write and manipulate files in various modes (e.g. read-only, write-only, and read-write). The open() function returns a file object, which you can use to perform various operations on the file, such as reading or writing its contents. Additionally, the os and shutil modules provide additional functionality for working with files and directories, such as creating, renaming, and deleting files and directories, and navigating the file system.

9.1 Operations on Files

There are several operations you can perform on files in Python, some of the most common include:

1. **Reading a file:** You can use the read() method of a file object to read the entire contents of a file into a string, or you can use the readline() method to read individual lines of the file.

2. **Writing to a file:** You can use the write() method of a file object to write a string to a file. If you want to add new content to an existing file, you can open the file in "append" mode.
3. **Updating a file:** You can use the seek() method of a file object to move the file pointer to a specific position in the file, and then use the write() method to overwrite the contents of the file at that position.
4. **Closing a file:** Once you have finished working with a file, you should close it using the close() method of the file object.
5. **Renaming and deleting a file:** Python provides functions like os.rename(), os.remove() etc. which can be used to rename and delete files.
6. **File handling** can also be done using context manager with the help of "with" statement, this will automatically close the file when the block of code is exited.
7. **Iterating through the file:** The for loop can be used to iterate through the lines of a file.
8. **Copying a file:** shutil.copy2() function can be used to copy a file from one location to another, while preserving the metadata of the original file.
9. **Moving a file:** shutil.move() can be used to move a file from one location to another.

These are just a few examples of the many operations you can perform on files in Python. The os and shutil modules provide additional functionality for working with files and directories, such as creating, renaming, and deleting files and directories, and navigating the file system.

9.1.1 Opening a File

In Python, the built-in open() function is used to open a file. The basic syntax for opening a file is:

```
file_object = open(file_name, mode)
```

where file_name is the name of the file you want to open, and mode is a string that specifies the mode in which the file should be opened. The mode can be "r" for reading, "w" for writing, "a" for appending, and "b" for binary mode.

Here is an example of how to open a file for reading in Python:

```
file_object = open("example.txt", "r")
```

This will open the file "example.txt" in read mode and return a file object, which can be used to read the contents of the file. Once you are finished working with the file, you should close it using the close() method of the file object.

Here is an example of how to read the contents of a file, and then close it:

Code 9.1: A program to read the content of a file.

```
file_object = open("example.txt", "r")
print(file_object.read())
file_object.close()
```

You can also use context manager to open a file and this will automatically close the file when the block of code is exited.

```
with open("example.txt", "r") as file_object:
    print(file_object.read())
```

It is important to note that the file you are trying to open should exist in the directory from where the python script is running otherwise it will raise FileNotFoundError.

9.1.2 File Modes

File modes in Python are used to specify the type of access a file should have when it is opened. The mode can be specified as a string using the following characters:

Here is a table of the different file modes:

Table 9.1: Different modes of file

Mode	Description
'r'	Open text file for reading. (default)
'w'	Open the file for writing. Creates the file if it does not exist or truncates the file if it exists.
'x'	Open the file for exclusive creation. If the file already exists, raises a FileExistsError.
'a'	Open the file for writing. Creates the file if it does not exist. The pointer is placed at the end of the file. If the file exists, data is appended.

Mode	Description
'b'	Binary mode
't'	Text mode (default)

You can also use these modes in combination, for example 'rb' f or reading a binary file or 'w+' for both reading and writing.

9.1.3 File object Attributes

File objects in Python have several attributes that provide information about the file or allow you to change the file's settings. Here are some common attributes:

1. **name:** The name of the file that the file object is associated with.
2. **mode:** The mode in which the file was opened, as a string (e.g. 'r', 'w', 'a').
3. **closed:** A Boolean indicating whether the file is closed.
4. **encoding:** The name of the encoding used for the file, if it was opened in text mode.
5. **newlines**: The newline mode used for the file, if it was opened in text mode.

Here is an example of how to use some of these attributes:

```
f = open("example.txt", "r")
print(f.name)
f.close()
```

This will print the name of the file, "example.txt"

9.1.4 File Encoding

File encoding in Python refers to the way in which characters are represented in a file. The most common file encodings used in Python are UTF-8 and UTF-16. UTF-8 is a variable-width encoding that can represent all Unicode characters, while UTF-16 uses a fixed-width encoding and requires 2 bytes per character. When opening a file in Python, you can specify the encoding using the encoding parameter of the open() function. For example, to open a file named "example. txt" using UTF-8 encoding, you would use the following code:

```
with open("example.txt", "r", encoding="utf-8") as f:
    content = f.read()
```

If you don't specify the encoding when opening a file, Python will try to detect the encoding automatically using a library called chardet. However, this method may not always be reliable, so it's a good practice to specify the encoding explicitly.

You can also use the io module to open a file with a specific encoding.

```
import io
with io.open("example.txt", "r", encoding="utf-8") as f:
    content = f.read()
```

It is important to note that if you are working with non-English text, you should always specify the encoding of the file to ensure that the text is displayed correctly.

9.1.5 Closing a File

In Python, a file must be closed after it is no longer needed to free up system resources and to ensure that any changes made to the file are properly saved. There are two ways to close a file in Python: using the close() method and using the with statement. The close() method is used to close a file that was opened using the open() function. For example, the following code opens a file named "example.txt" for reading, reads its contents, and then closes the file:

```
f = open("example.txt", "r")
content = f.read()
f.close()
```

It's important to note that if you forget to close a file, or if an error occurs while the file is open, the file may be left in an inconsistent state and your data may be lost. A more recommended way of opening and closing files is using the with statement. The with statement automatically takes care of closing the file, even if an error occurs. Here's an example:

```
with open("example.txt", "r") as f:
    content = f.read()
```

The file will be closed automatically when the block of code indented under the with statement is finished executing. It is worth noting that the file object returned by the open() function also has a __exit__() method which is called when the block of code indented under the with statement is finished executing, the __exit__() method will then call the close() method.

9.2 write() and read() Methods

In Python, the write() and read() methods are used to read and write data to and from files.

The write() method is used to write data to a file. It takes a string as an argument and writes it to the file. For example, the following code opens a file named "example.txt" for writing, writes some text to the file, and then closes the file:

9.2.1 Writing to a File

In Python, you can write to a file using the write() method of the file object. The write() method takes a string as an argument and writes it to the file.

Here's an example of writing to a new file "example.txt"

```
with open("example.txt", "a") as f:
    f.write("This is an additional line.")
```

You can also write multiple lines to a file by passing a list of strings to the writelines() method. It writes each element of the list as a separate line in the file.

```
lines = ["Line 1", "Line 2", "Line 3"]
with open("example.txt", "w") as f:
    f.writelines(line + '\n' for line in lines)
```

It's worth noting that the write() method writes the data as bytes, not as a string, so if you want to write string data, you need to encode it first using the encode() method.

```
with open("example.txt", "w", encoding="utf-8") as f:
    f.write("Hello, World!")
```

You can also use io module to write file in python

```
import io
with io.open("example.txt", "w", encoding="utf-8") as f:
    f.write("Hello, World!")
```

9.2.2 Reading from a File

In Python, you can read from a file using the read() method of the file object. The read() method reads the entire contents of the file and returns it as a string.

Here's an example of reading the contents of a file "example.txt":

```
with open("example.txt", "r") as f:
    content = f.read()
    print(content)
```

You can also read the file in chunks, rather than reading the entire file at once, by passing an argument to the read() method. The argument is the number of bytes to read each time. For example, the following code reads the first 100 bytes of the file:

```
with open("example.txt", "r") as f:
    content = f.read(100)
    print(content)
```

9.3 Python File Methods

In Python, there are several built-in methods that you can use to work with files:

Table 9.2 : Bulit in File Methods

Method Name	Description
open(file, mode)	This function is used to open a file and returns a file object. The file parameter is the name of the file, and the mode parameter is used to specify the mode in which the file should be opened, such as 'r' for reading, 'w' for writing, and 'a' for appending.
file.read([size])	This method reads at most size bytes from the file. If the size parameter is not specified, it will read the entire file.
file.readline()	This method reads a single line from the file.
file.readlines()	This method reads all the lines of the file and returns them as a list.
file.write(string)	This method writes the contents of the string to the file.
file.writelines(list)	This method writes a list of strings to the file.
file.seek(offset[, whence])	This method changes the file position to the given offset. The whence parameter is optional and defaults to 0, which means absolute file positioning.
file.tell()	This method returns the current file position.
file.close()	This method closes the file.

When you are done working with a file, it is important to close it using the file.close() method to free up system resources.

It's important to note that, python have other library like pandas and numpy that have their own file read and write functionality. They are more powerful and flexible than the built-in python file methods

You can use it like this:

```
import pandas as pd
df = pd.read_csv('file.csv')
df.to_csv('newfile.csv', index=False)
```

9.4 tell() and seek() Methods

The tell() method in Python returns the current position of the file pointer. This is an integer value that represents the number of bytes from the beginning of the file.

The seek() method in Python allows you to move the file pointer to a specific position. You can specify the position as an integer value, measured in bytes from the beginning of the file. The method takes two arguments: the first argument is the position to move the pointer to, and the second argument is an optional value that specifies how to interpret the first argument.

For example, the following code opens a file, reads the current position, moves the pointer to a new position, and then reads the new position:

```
f = open("example.txt", "r")
print(f.tell()) # prints 0
f.seek(5)
print(f.tell()) # prints 5
f.close()
```

It's important to note that after moving the pointer, it's possible to read or write the file from the new position.

9.5 Renaming and Deleting Files

In Python, you can rename and delete files using the os module. To rename a file, you can use the os.rename() function, which takes the current file name and the new file name as its arguments. For example:

```
import os
os.rename("current_file.txt", "new_file.txt")
```

To delete a file, you can use the os.remove() function, which takes the file name as its argument. For example:

```
import os
os.remove("file_to_delete.txt")
```

It's also worth noting that there is also shutil module which also have similar functionality such as shutil.move(src, dst) and shutil.rmtree(path, ignore_errors=False, onerror=None) which can be useful in some cases.

9.5.1 Rename() Method

The rename() method in python is used to rename a file or directory. It is a method of the os module and takes two arguments: the current name of the file or directory and the new name. For example, to rename a file "old_file.txt" to "new_file.txt", you would use the following code:

```
import os
os.rename("old_file.txt", "new_file.txt")
```

It also can be used with os.path.join() method to rename files in a specific directory.

```
import os
os.rename(os.path.join(directory, 'old_file.txt'), os.path.join(directory, 'new_file.txt'))
```

Note that this method will raise a FileNotFoundError if the file or directory you are trying to rename does not exist, or a PermissionError if you do not have permission to rename the file or directory.

9.5.2 Remove() Method

The remove() method in Python is a built-in method for lists that can be used to remove an item from a list. The method takes a single argument, which is the item to be removed from the list. If the item is not present in the list, the method raises a ValueError exception.

Syntax : list.remove(item)

For example:

```
numbers = [1, 2, 3, 4, 5]
numbers.remove(3)
print(numbers) # Output: [1, 2, 4, 5]
```

In this example, the remove() method is used to remove the value 3 from the list numbers. After the method is called, the list contains the values 1, 2, 4, and 5, and the value 3 is no longer present in the list.

9.6 Directories in Python

In Python, a directory is a file system folder that contains other files or directories. Python provides several built-in modules, such as os and os.path, that make it easy to interact with the file system and manipulate directories.

The os module provides a way to interact with the underlying operating system, including creating, moving, and deleting files and directories. The os.path module provides additional functionality for working with file and directory paths, such as checking whether a path is a file or a directory, and joining multiple paths together.

With the os and os.path modules, you can perform various operations on directories in Python such as:

- Creating new directories
- Changing the current working directory
- Listing the contents of a directory
- Removing a directory
- Renaming a directory
- Checking if a directory exists

These modules are a powerful tool for automating common file and directory tasks, and for creating scripts that manipulate the file system in various ways.

9.6.1 mkdir() Method

The os.mkdir() method in Python is a function that creates a new directory with the specified name. It takes one argument, which is the name of the directory to be created.

Syntax : os.mkdir(path, mode = 0o777, *, dir_fd = None)

The path parameter is required, and it specifies the name of the directory to be created. The mode parameter is an optional argument that specifies the permissions mode for the new directory, and the default value is 0o777. The dir_fd parameter is used to specify a file descriptor for the parent directory. For example:

```
import os
os.mkdir("new_directory")
```

This example creates a new directory called "new_directory" in the current working directory. If the directory already exists, os.mkdir() will raise a FileExistsError exception.

It's important to note that the os.mkdir() method creates only one new directory at a time, If you need to create multiple directories at once you can use os.makedirs() method.

9.6.2 chdir() Method

The os.chdir() method in Python is a function that changes the current working directory. It takes one argument, which is the path to the new directory.

Syntax : os.chdir(path)

The path parameter is required, and it specifies the path to the new directory. The method changes the current working directory to the specified path. For example:

```
import os
os.chdir("/new_directory")
```

This example changes the current working directory to "/new_directory"

It's important to note that the os.chdir() method only change the current working directory for the process that calls it. It does not affect the current working directory of other processes or of the terminal where the script is run. Also, if the specified directory does not exist, the os.chdir() method will raise a FileNotFoundError exception.

9.6.3 getcwd() Method

getcwd() is a method in the os module in Python that stands for "Get Current Working Directory". It returns a string representing the current working directory (i.e., the directory in which the Python process is running). Example usage:

```
import os
current_dir = os.getcwd()
print(current_dir)
```

9.6.4 rmdir() Method

rmdir() is a method in the os module in Python that stands for “Remove Directory”. It is used to remove an empty directory. If the directory is not empty, the method will raise an error. Example usage:

```
import os
os.rmdir(“path/to/directory”)
```

Note: The directory to be removed must be empty, otherwise, a FileNotFoundError or OSError will be raised.

9.6.5 listdir() Method

listdir() is a method in the os module in Python that returns a list of filenames in the specified directory. If no directory is specified, it defaults to the current working directory. Example usage:

```
import os
files_and_dirs = os.listdir(“path/to/directory”)
print(files_and_dirs)
```

The resulting list includes both files and directories, so to list only the files or only the directories, you can use additional filtering logic on the list returned by listdir().

9.7 Python Directory Methods

In Python, the os module provides a number of methods for working with directories. Here are some of the most commonly used methods:

Table 9.3 : Directory Methods in Python

Method	Description
os.mkdir(path)	Creates a new directory at the specified path.
os.rmdir(path)	Removes the directory at the specified path (the directory must be empty).

Method	Description
os.chdir(path)	Changes the current working directory to the specified path.
os.getcwd()	Returns a string representing the current working directory.
os.listdir(path)	Returns a list of filenames in the specified directory (defaults to the current working directory if no path is specified).
os.scandir(path)	Returns an iterator of DirEntry objects representing entries in the specified directory (similar to listdir(), but faster and provides more information about each entry).
os.makedirs(path)	Recursively creates directories, including any intermediate ones that do not exist.
os.removedirs(path)	Recursively removes directories, including any intermediate ones that are now empty.
os.stat(path)	Returns information about the specified file or directory as a stat_result object.
os.path.isdir(path)	os.path.isdir(path)

9.8 Summary

In this chapter, we delve into the subject of data files. We cover the various techniques for handling files and directories in Python, along with the practical applications of each method. Topics include creating and opening files, operating in different modes such as reading and writing, as well as methods for renaming, deleting, creating directories, changing directories, and removing directories.

Review Questions

1. What is a file in Python?
2. How do you open a file in Python and what modes are available?
3. What is the difference between read and write mode in Python file handling?
4. How do you read the contents of a file in Python?
5. How do you write data to a file in Python?
6. What is the difference between write and append mode in Python file handling?
7. How do you close a file in Python?
8. What is the os module in Python and how is it used for file handling?
9. How do you rename a file in Python?

10. How do you delete a file in Python?
11. Which of the following is not a method for file handling in Python?
    (a) open()
    (b) close()
    (c) read()
    (d) writeLine()
12. Which of the following is true about directories in Python?
    (a) Directories can only contain files and not other directories
    (b) The os module in Python can be used to create and delete directories
    (c) Directories in Python cannot be nested
    (d) Directories in Python can only be created in the root directory

10

Classes and Objects

Highlights

- Object-Oriented Programming Methodologies
- Designing Classes
- Creating Objects
- Accessing Attributes
- Built - in Class Attributes
- Garbage Collection

Object-Oriented Programming (OOP) is a programming methodology that revolves around the concept of objects, which are instances of classes. In Python, you can use OOP to create classes that encapsulate data and behavior. A class defines the attributes and methods that objects of that class will have. Attributes are the data or properties of an object, while methods are the functions or behaviors that the object can perform.

To create a class in Python, you use the "class" keyword, followed by the name of the class and a colon. Within the class, you define attributes and methods using instance variables and instance methods. Instance variables are variables that are specific to each object of the class, while instance methods are methods that can be called on each object of the class.

In Python, you can also use inheritance to create subclasses that inherit attributes and methods from a parent class. This allows you to reuse code and create hierarchies of classes that share common behavior. OOP in Python can be used to create complex programs and libraries, as well as to model real-world objects and systems.

Object-Oriented Programming Methodologies:

- **Class:** A blueprint or template for creating objects that share similar attributes and behaviors.
- **Object:** An instance of a class that has its own set of attributes and methods.
- **Inheritance:** A way to create new classes based on existing classes, inheriting their attributes and methods.
- **Polymorphism:** The ability of objects to take on different forms or behave in different ways depending on the context.
- **Encapsulation:** The practice of hiding the internal details of an object and exposing only the necessary information through methods.
- **Abstraction:** The process of reducing complexity by hiding unnecessary details, allowing you to focus on the essential features of an object or system.

Classes and objects are the fundamental building blocks of object-oriented programming (OOP) in Python.

A class is a blueprint or template for creating objects, which can contain data (attributes) and code (methods) that act on that data. Classes provide a way to structure the data and behavior of similar objects, making it easier to create and manage those objects.

An object is an instance of a class, created at runtime, with its own set of attributes and methods. Objects are used to model real-world entities and their behavior, making it easier to represent and manipulate complex data and logic in a program.

In Python, you can define a class using the class keyword, followed by the name of the class, and then the class definition inside a code block. You can define the attributes and methods of a class, and when you create an object from a class, it will inherit all of the attributes and methods defined in that class.

Here's a simple example to illustrate the concept of classes and objects in Python:

```
class Car:
    def __init__(self, make, model, year):
        self.make = make
        self.model = model
        self.year = year

    def honk(self):
        print("Beep beep!")

# Create an object of the Car class
my_car = Car("Toyota", "Camry", 2020)

# Access attributes of the object
print(my_car.make)
print(my_car.model)
print(my_car.year)

# Call a method of the object
my_car.honk()
```

In this example, we define a class Car with three attributes (make, model, and year) and a single method (honk). We then create an object my_car from the Car class, and access its attributes and call its methods.

10.1 Designing Classes

In Python, classes are used to define custom data structures that can be used to model real-world objects and their behavior. A class is defined using the class keyword, followed by the name of the class, and a colon. The body of the class is indented, and it can contain methods (functions that are associated with the class) and attributes (data that is associated with the class).

Here is a simple example of a class in Python:

Code 10.1 designing class in Python

```
class Dog:
    def __init__(self, name, breed):
        self.name = name
        self.breed = breed
    def bark(self):
        print("Woof!")
```

In this example, the Dog class has two attributes name and breed, and one method bark(). The special method __init__ is a constructor that is called when a new instance of the class is created. The self parameter refers to the instance of the class and is used to access attributes and methods.

10.2 Creating Objects

In Python, objects are instances of classes and represent real-world entities and their behavior. To create an object, you need to call the constructor of the class. The constructor is a special method called __init__, which is automatically invoked when you create an object.

Here's an example of how you can create an object in Python:

Code 10.2 creating an object in Python

```
class Dog:
    def __init__(self, name, breed):
        self.name = name
        self.breed = breed

    def bark(self):
        print("Woof!")

dog = Dog("Rufus", "Labrador")
```

In this example, we define a class called Dog with a constructor __init__ that takes two parameters name and breed. We then create an instance of the Dog class by calling Dog("Rufus", "Labrador"). This creates a new object dog and initializes its name and breed attributes.

Code 10.3 access the attributes of an object using dot notation

```
print(dog.name) # Outputs: "Rufus"
print(dog.breed) # Outputs: "Labrador"
```

You can also call the methods of an object in the same way:

```
dog.bark() # Outputs: "Woof!"
```

This is just a simple example of how you can create objects in Python. You can define more complex classes with multiple attributes, methods, and inheritance to model real-world objects and their behavior.

10.2.1 Class Variable

In Python, a class variable is a variable that is shared by all instances (objects) of a class. It is a variable that is defined within the class, but outside of any methods. Class variables are accessed using the class name, rather than an instance of the class.

Class variables are useful for storing data that is common to all instances of a class, such as a default value or a constant. They can be modified by any instance of the class, but the changes will be visible to all instances of the class.

Code 10.4 Illustration of class variable

```
class MyClass:
    class_variable = 0
    def __init__(self, instance_variable):
        self.instance_variable = instance_variable
        MyClass.class_variable += 1
    def print_variables(self):
        print(f'Instance variable: {self.instance_variable}")
        print(f'Class variable: {MyClass.class_variable}")
```

10.2.2 Instance Variable

In Python, an instance variable is a variable that is unique to each instance (object) of a class. It is a variable that is defined within the class, but inside a method, usually the __init__() method, which gets called when a new object is created. Each instance of the class has its own set of instance variables.

Instance variables are used to store data that is specific to each instance of the class, such as the name or age of a person. Instance variables are accessed using the self keyword, which refers to the instance of the class.

Code 10.5 Illustration of class with instance variables

```
class Person:
    def __init__(self, name, age):
        self.name = name
        self.age = age
    def say_hello(self):
       print(f"Hello, my name is {self.name} and I'm {self.age} years old.")
```

In this example, name and age are instance variables that are initialized with the values passed in as arguments to the __init__() method. The say_hello() method uses these instance variables to print out a message.

To create objects from this class and access the instance variables, you would do the following:

Code 10.6 Illustration of class with instance variables

```
person1 = Person("Alice", 30)
person2 = Person("Bob", 25)
person1.say_hello() # Output: Hello, my name is Alice and I'm 30 years old.
person2.say_hello() # Output: Hello, my name is Bob and I'm 25 years old.
```

In this example, person1 and person2 are two different instances of the Person class, and they each have their own set of instance variables name and age. The say_hello() method prints out the values of these instance variables for the given object.

10.3 Types of Methods

In Python, there are three types of methods that can be defined within a class:

1. **Instance Methods:** These are the most common type of methods and are associated with the object of a class. They take self as the first parameter and are used to modify the object's state or behavior.
2. **Class Methods:** These methods are associated with the class and can be called on the class itself, rather than an instance of the class. They take cls as the first parameter and are used to modify the class's state or behavior.
3. **Static Methods:** These methods are not associated with either the class or the instance of the class. They take no special parameters (self or cls) and are used for utility functions that do not depend on the class's state or behavior.

Code 10.7 Illustration of class method

```
class MyClass:
    class_variable = 0
    def __init__(self, instance_variable):
        self.instance_variable = instance_variable
        MyClass.class_variable += 1
    def instance_method(self):
        print(f"This is an instance method. Instance variable: {self.instance_
variable}")
    @classmethod
    def class_method(cls):
        print(f"This is a class method. Class variable: {cls.class_variable}")
    @staticmethod
    def static_method():
        print("This is a static method.")
```

In this example, instance_method is an instance method, class_method is a class method, and static_method is a static method. instance_method takes self as the first parameter, class_method takes cls as the first parameter and is decorated with @classmethod, and static_method takes no special parameters and is decorated with @staticmethod.

Code 10.7 Illustration of call class method

```
obj = MyClass("object")
obj.instance_method() # Output: This is an instance method. Instance variable: object
MyClass.class_method() # Output: This is a class method. Class variable: 1
MyClass.static_method() # Output: This is a static method.
```

In this example, obj is an instance of the MyClass class, and we call the instance_method method on it. We also call the class_method and static_method methods on the MyClass class itself.

10.4 Access Specifiers in Python

In Python, access specifiers are used to restrict access to class attributes and methods from outside the class. There are no true access specifiers in Python like in other object-oriented programming languages, such as private, protected, and public. However, Python provides a convention of using underscores to indicate the intended visibility of a class member. Here are the different types of access specifiers in Python:

1. **Public:** These are class members that are intended to be accessible from outside the class. There are no special syntax rules to define public members. They are just defined without any leading underscores.
2. **Protected:** These are class members that are intended to be accessed only within the class and its subclasses. In Python, there is no true protected access specifier, but the convention is to use a single leading underscore to indicate that a member is intended to be protected.
3. **Private:** These are class members that are intended to be accessed only within the class. In Python, there is no true private access specifier, but the convention is to use a double leading underscore to indicate that a member is intended to be private.

Code 10.8 Illustration of access specifiers in python

```
class MyClass:
    def __init__(self):
        self.public_member = "public"
        self._protected_member = "protected"
        self.__private_member = "private"
```

```
    def get_private_member(self):
        return self.__private_member
```

In this example, public_member is a public member, _protected_member is a protected member, and __private_member is a private member. The get_private_member method is used to retrieve the value of the private member.

Code 10.9 To access these members from outside the class

```
obj = MyClass()
print(obj.public_member)          # Output: public
print(obj._protected_member)      # Output: protected
print(obj.get_private_member())   # Output: private
```

In this example, public_member and _protected_member can be accessed directly from outside the class, while __private_member is accessed using the get_private_member method. However, it's important to note that these are just conventions, and there is nothing stopping a user from accessing or modifying these members directly, even if they are intended to be protected or private.

10.5 Accessing Attributes

In Python, you can access the attributes of an object using dot notation. The syntax is object_name.attribute_name.

Here's an example:

Code 10.10 accessing attributes in Python

```
class Dog:
    def __init__(self, name, breed):
        self.name = name
        self.breed = breed
    def bark(self):
        print("Woof!")
dog = Dog("Rufus", "Labrador")
print(dog.name) # Outputs: "Rufus"
print(dog.breed) # Outputs: "Labrador"
```

In this example, the Dog class has two attributes name and breed. We create an instance of the Dog class and store it in the variable dog. To access the attributes of the dog object, we use dot notation dog.name and dog.breed.

You can also access the attributes of an object dynamically using the getattr function. The syntax is getattr(object_name, attribute_name). For example:

Code 10.11 accessing attributes using getattr function

```
name = getattr(dog, "name")
breed = getattr(dog, "breed")
print(name) # Outputs: "Rufus"
print(breed) # Outputs: "Labrador"
```

The getattr function takes two arguments: the object and the name of the attribute you want to access. If the attribute exists, it returns the value of the attribute. If the attribute does not exist, it returns an AttributeError. You can also provide a default value to be returned in case the attribute does not exist, by passing a third argument to getattr.

10.6 The Class Program

A class program in Python defines a custom data structure that can be used to model real-world objects and their behavior. Here is an example of a class program in Python:

Code 10.12 A class program in Python

```
class Car:
    def __init__(self, make, model, year):
        self.make = make
        self.model = model
        self.year = year
    def honk(self):
        print("Beep Beep!")
car = Car("Toyota", "Camry", 2020)
print(car.make) # Outputs: "Toyota"
print(car.model) # Outputs: "Camry"
print(car.year) # Outputs: 2020
car.honk() # Outputs: "Beep Beep!"
```

In this example, we define a class called Car with a constructor __init__ that takes three parameters make, model, and year. The constructor sets these parameters as attributes of the Car class. We also have a method honk that outputs "Beep Beep!" when called.

We then create an instance of the Car class and store it in the variable car. To access the attributes and call the methods of the car object, we use dot notation.

10.6.1 Using a Class with Input

In Python, you can use a class with user input by taking input from the user and passing it as arguments to the class constructor. Here's an example:

Code 10.13 A class with user input

```
class Dog:
    def __init__(self, name, breed):
        self.name = name
        self.breed = breed
    def bark(self):
        print("Woof!")
name = input("Enter dog name: ")
breed = input("Enter dog breed: ")
dog = Dog(name, breed)
print(dog.name)
print(dog.breed)
dog.bark()
```

In this example, we use the input function to take user input for the dog's name and breed. The user inputs are then passed as arguments to the Dog class constructor when creating a new instance of the class. The rest of the program works the same as before, accessing the attributes and calling the method of the dog object.

You can use this pattern to create class instances with user input in any Python program. Just make sure to handle any exceptions or errors that might occur, such as invalid input format, to ensure the stability and reliability of your program.

10.6.2 A Class Program with Computations

A class program with computations in Python is a program that uses a custom data structure defined using a class to perform computations. The class can have attributes and methods that are used to store and manipulate data, as well as perform operations and computations on the data.

For example, you can create a class that represents a circle and has attributes for the radius of the circle, as well as methods to calculate the area and circumference of the circle.

Code 10.14 A class program with computations in Python

```
class Circle:
    pi = 3.14
    def __init__(self, radius):
        self.radius = radius
    def area(self):
        return Circle.pi * (self.radius ** 2)
radius = float(input("Enter the radius of the circle: "))
circle = Circle(radius)
print("The area of the circle is", circle.area())
```

In this example, we define a class Circle with a class attribute pi set to 3.14. The class also has a constructor __init__ that takes a radius argument and sets it as an attribute of the Circle class. We also have a method area that calculates and returns the area of the circle using the formula pi * r^2.

We then create an instance of the Circle class and store it in the variable circle. We use the input function to take user input for the radius of the circle. The input is then converted to a float and passed as an argument to the Circle class constructor.

Finally, we call the area method on the circle object to calculate the area of the circle and print the result.

10.7 Editing Class Attributes

Editing class attributes in Python refers to the process of changing the value of an attribute that is associated with a class. Class attributes are defined in the class definition and are shared by all instances of the class.

In Python, you can edit class attributes by directly modifying the attribute value on an instance of the class. This means that you can change the value of an attribute for a specific instance of the class, without affecting the value of that attribute for other instances of the class or for the class definition itself.

Code 10.15 editing class attributes in Python

```
class Dog:
    def __init__(self, name, breed):
        self.name = name
        self.breed = breed
    def bark(self):
        print("Woof!")
dog = Dog("Buddy", "Labrador")
print(dog.name)
print(dog.breed)
dog.name = "Rufus"
dog.breed = "Golden Retriever"
print(dog.name)
print(dog.breed)
```

In this example, we create an instance of the Dog class and store it in the dog variable. We then print the original name and breed of the dog, which are "Buddy" and "Labrador".

Next, we modify the name and breed attributes of the dog object by directly assigning new values to them. Finally, we print the updated name and breed of the dog, which are "Rufus" and "Golden Retriever".

Note that the changes we make to the attributes of an instance of the class only affect that particular instance, and do not affect other instances or the class definition itself. This allows you to have different instances of the same class with different attribute values.

10.8 Built-in Class Attributes

In Python, there are several built-in class attributes that you can use to access information about a class or an instance of a class. Some of the most commonly used built-in class attributes are:

1. **__dict__**: A dictionary that contains the namespace of an object. It stores the object's attributes and their values.
2. **__doc__**: A string that contains the documentation for a class or an object.
3. **__name__**: A string that contains the name of the class or the object.
4. **__module__**: A string that contains the name of the module where the class or the object is defined.
5. **__class__**: A reference to the class that an instance of a class belongs to.

For example, consider the following class:

Code 10.16 built in attributes in Python

```
class Dog:
    species = "Canis lupus familiaris"

    def __init__(self, name, breed):
        self.name = name
        self.breed = breed

    def bark(self):
        print("Woof!")

dog = Dog("Buddy", "Labrador")

print(dog.__dict__)
print(dog.__doc__)
print(dog.__name__)
print(dog.__module__)
print(dog.__class__)
```

In this example, we create an instance of the Dog class and store it in the dog variable. Then, we use the built-in class attributes __dict__, __doc__, __name__, __module__, and __class__ to access information about the dog instance.

The output of this code will be a dictionary that contains the attributes and values of the dog instance, a string that contains the documentation for the Dog class (which is empty in this case), a string that contains the name of the dog instance (which is not defined), a string that contains the name of the module where the Dog class is defined, and a reference to the Dog class itself.

10.9 Garbage Collection/Destroying Objects

In Python, memory management is handled automatically by the Python interpreter, using a mechanism called "garbage collection". The garbage collector periodically frees up memory that is no longer being used by the program.

When an object is no longer needed, the Python interpreter automatically marks the object as "unreachable" and the memory occupied by the object becomes eligible for garbage collection. When the next garbage collection cycle occurs, the memory occupied by the unreachable object is freed up.

In general, you do not need to worry about destroying objects in Python, as the garbage collector takes care of it automatically. However, there may be times when you want to explicitly release an object's memory before the next garbage collection cycle.

To do this, you can use the del statement in Python. The del statement removes the reference to an object, making the object eligible for garbage collection. For example:

```
dog = Dog("Buddy", "Labrador")
del dog
```

In this example, we create an instance of the Dog class and store it in the dog variable. Then, we use the del statement to remove the reference to the dog instance, making it eligible for garbage collection.

Note that removing a reference to an object does not immediately free up the memory occupied by the object. The memory occupied by the object will be freed up during the next garbage collection cycle.

10.10 Summary

In this chapter, we covered the basics of designing classes in Python. A class is a blueprint for creating objects, which can be used to encapsulate data and behavior. We learned how to create objects from a class by calling the class as if it were a function. We also learned how to access the attributes of an object using dot notation. In addition to user-defined attributes, Python has several built-in class attributes that can be used to access information about a class or an object. These built-in attributes include __dict__, __doc__, __name__, __module__, and __class__. Finally, we learned about garbage collection in Python, which is a mechanism for freeing up memory that is no longer being used by the program. The Python interpreter automatically frees up memory that is no longer being used through a mechanism called "garbage collection", although it is possible to explicitly release an object's memory by using the del statement.

Review Questions

1. What is a class in Python?
2. How do you create an object from a class in Python?
3. How do you access the attributes of an object in Python?
4. What are some built-in class attributes in Python?
5. What is the purpose of garbage collection in Python?
6. How does Python handle memory management?
7. Can you explicitly release an object's memory in Python?
8. What is the difference between a class and an object in Python?
9. How do you access the documentation of a class in Python?
10. What is the purpose of the __dict__ built-in class attribute in Python?
11. What is the purpose of the __init__ method in a Python class?
    A. To initialize the class
    B. To call other methods within the class
    C. To specify the attributes of an object
12. What is the purpose of garbage collection in Python?
    A. To free up memory that is no longer being used by the program
    B. To increase the speed of the program
    C. To reduce the memory usage of the program

11

Inheritance

Highlights

- Python Single Inheritance
- Python Multiple Inheritance
- Python Multilevel Inheritance
- Method Overriding in Python
- Special Functions in Python

Inheritance is a concept in object-oriented programming (OOP) where a class can inherit properties and methods from a parent class. This allows you to create new classes that are related to existing classes, and to reuse or extend the existing code. The new class is called the derived class or subclass, and the existing class is called the base class or superclass.

In Python, inheritance is implemented using the class inheritance syntax. A subclass is defined by including the name of the parent class in parentheses after the class name, like this:

```
class DerivedClass(BaseClass):
    # subclass code here
```

The subclass inherits all the attributes and methods of the parent class, and can add new attributes or override existing ones. This makes it possible to reuse and extend code, and to create more specialized classes that are based on a common base class.

Inheritance is a powerful feature of OOP that allows for code reuse and modularity. It makes it possible to define common functionality once in a base class, and then reuse that functionality in multiple derived classes.

11.1 Python Single Inheritance

Single inheritance is a type of inheritance in object-oriented programming (OOP) where a subclass inherits properties and methods from a single parent class. In Python, single inheritance is achieved by defining a subclass and specifying the parent class in parentheses after the subclass name.

Code 11.1 single inheritance in Python

```
class Animal:
    def __init__(self, name, species):
        self.name = name
        self.species = species
    def make_sound(self):
        print("Some generic animal sound")
class Dog(Animal):
    def __init__(self, name, breed):
        Animal.__init__(self, name, species="Dog")
        self.breed = breed
    def make_sound(self):
        print("Woof woof!")
dog = Dog("Max", "Labrador")
print(dog.name)
print(dog.species)
print(dog.breed)
dog.make_sound()
```

In this example, the Dog class inherits from the Animal class. This means that the Dog class has access to all the attributes and methods of the Animal class, including the name and species attributes and the make_sound method. The Dog class can also add its own attributes and methods, such as the breed attribute and its own implementation of the make_sound method.

11.2 Python Multiple Inheritance

Multiple inheritance is a type of inheritance in object-oriented programming (OOP) where a class inherits properties and methods from multiple parent classes. In Python, multiple inheritance is achieved by defining a class and specifying multiple parent classes in parentheses after the class name, separated by commas.

Code 11.2 multiple inheritance in Python

```
class Person:
    def __init__(self, name, age):
        self.name = name
        self.age = age
    def say_hello(self):
        print(f"Hello, my name is {self.name}")
class Student:
    def __init__(self, student_id):
        self.student_id = student_id
    def enroll(self):
        print(f"Enrolling student with ID {self.student_id}")
class Teacher(Person, Student):
    def __init__(self, name, age, teacher_id):
        Person.__init__(self, name, age)
        Student.__init__(self, teacher_id)
        self.teacher_id = teacher_id
    def teach(self):
        print(f"Teacher {self.name} is teaching")
teacher = Teacher("Jane Doe", 35, 12345)
print(teacher.name)
```

```
print(teacher.age)
print(teacher.student_id)
print(teacher.teacher_id)
teacher.say_hello()
teacher.enroll()
teacher.teach()
```

In this example, the Teacher class inherits from both the Person and Student classes. This means that the Teacher class has access to all the attributes and methods of both the Person and Student classes, including the name, age, student_id, and enroll methods. The Teacher class can also add its own attributes and methods, such as the teacher_id attribute and the teach method.

It's important to note that when multiple inheritance is used, the order of the parent classes in the class definition can matter. If there are conflicts between the parent classes, the first parent class in the list will take precedence. This is known as the method resolution order (MRO) in Python.

11.3 Python Multilevel Inheritance

Multilevel inheritance is a type of inheritance in object-oriented programming (OOP) where a class inherits properties and methods from a parent class, which itself inherits properties and methods from a grandparent class. In other words, the inheritance is hierarchical and passes down from one generation to the next.

Code 11.3 multilevel inheritance in Python

```
class Animal:
    def __init__(self, species):
        self.species = species
    def make_sound(self):
        print(f"{self.species} makes a sound")
class Mammal(Animal):
    def __init__(self, species, fur_color):
        Animal.__init__(self, species)
        self.fur_color = fur_color
```

```
    def have_fur(self):
        print(f"{self.species} has {self.fur_color} fur")
class Dog(Mammal):
    def __init__(self, breed, fur_color):
        Mammal.__init__(self, "Dog", fur_color)
        self.breed = breed
    def bark(self):
        print(f"{self.breed} barks")
dog = Dog("Labrador", "Golden")
print(dog.species)
print(dog.fur_color)
print(dog.breed)
dog.make_sound()
dog.have_fur()
dog.bark()
```

In this example, the Dog class inherits from the Mammal class, which in turn inherits from the Animal class. This creates a hierarchical inheritance structure where the Dog class has access to all the attributes and methods of both the Mammal and Animal classes, including the species, fur_color, make_sound, and have_fur methods. The Dog class can also add its own attributes and methods, such as the breed attribute and the bark method.

Multilevel inheritance allows for a more organized and reusable code structure, as properties and methods can be shared between classes in a hierarchical manner.

11.4 Method Overriding in Python

Method overriding is a feature in object-oriented programming (OOP) where a subclass provides a new implementation for a method that is already defined in its parent class. The method in the subclass has the same name, return type, and parameters as the method in the parent class, but the implementation is different.

In Python, method overriding is achieved by defining a method with the same name in the subclass as in the parent class. The new implementation in the subclass will override the implementation in the parent class for objects of the subclass.

Code 11.4 method overriding in Python

```
class Shape:
    def area(self):
        pass
class Square(Shape):
    def __init__(self, side):
        self.side = side
    def area(self):
        return self.side * self.side
square = Square(5)
print(square.area())
```

In this example, the Square class inherits from the Shape class. The Shape class has a area method that does not have an implementation. The Square class provides its own implementation for the area method by defining the method with the same name in the class and providing its own implementation. When the area method is called on a Square object, the implementation in the Square class is used instead of the one in the Shape class. This is an example of method overriding.

Method overriding is a powerful feature that allows subclasses to provide their own implementation for a method while still preserving the same interface as the parent class. This makes the code more flexible and reusable, as subclasses can inherit common properties and methods from the parent class but still have the ability to customize their behavior.

11.5 Special Functions in Python

In Python, special functions are a set of functions that have special behavior and are used in specific situations. Some of the most common special functions are:

1. **__init__**: The __init__ method is a special function that is called when an object is created from a class. It is used to initialize the object's attributes and can take arguments to set the values of those attributes.

2. **__str__**: The __str__ method is a special function that is used to return a string representation of an object. The string returned by __str__ is used when the print function is used on the object or when the str function is used to convert the object to a string.
3. **__repr__**: The __repr__ method is similar to the __str__ method, but is used to return a string representation of an object that can be used to recreate the object. The string returned by __repr__ is used when the repr function is used to convert the object to a string.
4. **__add__**: The __add__ method is used to define the behavior of the + operator when used on objects of the class. By defining __add__, you can specify how objects of the class should be added together.
5. **__len__**: The __len__ method is used to define the behavior of the len function when used on objects of the class. By defining __len__, you can specify how the length of an object should be calculated.
6. **__getitem__**: The __getitem__ method is used to define the behavior of the indexing operator [] when used on objects of the class. By defining __getitem__, you can specify how objects of the class should be indexed.
7. **__setitem__**: The __setitem__ method is used to define the behavior of the index assignment operator [] when used on objects of the class. By defining __setitem__, you can specify how objects of the class should be modified through indexing.

These special functions allow you to customize the behavior of your classes and make them more versatile. By using these functions, you can create objects that behave like built-in data types, such as strings and lists, and that can be used in a more intuitive and natural way.

11.6 Summary

Inheritance is a fundamental aspect of object-oriented programming in Python, which allows you to create new classes that inherit properties and behaviors from existing classes. The concept of inheritance allows for code reusability and modularity, making it easier to maintain and extend code over time. In Python, you can achieve inheritance through single inheritance, multiple inheritance, and multilevel inheritance. Single inheritance is when a class inherits properties and behaviors from a single parent class. Multiple inheritance is when a class inherits properties and behaviors from multiple parent classes. Multilevel inheritance is when a class inherits properties and behaviors from a parent class, which in turn inherits from another parent class. Method overriding is another important aspect of inheritance, where a subclass can provide its own implementation for a method defined in its parent class. Additionally, there are several special functions in Python, such as init, str, and repr, which have specific functionality and can be overridden in a subclass to customize its behavior. In conclusion, inheritance is a powerful feature in Python that allows you to create complex, hierarchical class structures with ease, while maintaining code reuse and modularity.

Review Questions

1. What is the purpose of Multiple Inheritance in Python?
2. Can a class inherit from multiple parent classes in Python?
3. What is the difference between Multiple Inheritance and Multilevel Inheritance?
4. How does Method Overriding work in Python?
5. Can you provide an example of Method Overriding in Python?
6. What are the Special Functions in Python, and how do they work?
7. Can you provide an example of the init special function in Python?
8. What is the purpose of the str special function in Python?
9. Can you explain the use of the repr special function in Python?
10. What is the role of the super() function in relation to Method Overriding in Python?
11. What is Multiple Inheritance in Python?
    (a) When a class inherits properties and behaviors from a single parent class
    (b) When a class inherits properties and behaviors from multiple parent classes
    (c) When a class inherits properties and behaviors from a parent class, which in turn inherits from another parent class
12. What is Method Overriding in Python?
    (a) The process of providing a new implementation for a method defined in a parent class
    (b) The process of calling a method from a parent class
    (c) The process of extending a method defined in a parent class

12

Python Operator Overloading

Highlights

- Overloading '+' Operator in Python
- Overloading '-' Operator in Python
- Overloading Bitwise Operators
- Overloading Relational Operators

Operator Overloading in Python is a mechanism that allows us to change the behavior of operators for instances of custom classes. This means that we can use the familiar mathematical and comparison operators (+, -, *, /, ==, !=, etc.) on instances of our own classes, and specify how these operators should behave for those instances. This allows us to write more natural and readable code, as well as make our classes more convenient to use. Operator Overloading is achieved through the use of special methods in Python, such as add, sub, mul, truediv, and others. By defining these special methods, we can specify how our objects should behave when they are subjected to these operators.

12.1 Overloading '+' Operator in Python

To overload the "+" operator in Python, we can define the add method in our custom class. The add method takes two arguments, self and other, and is responsible for returning the result of adding the two objects together.

Here's an example of how you might overload the "+" operator for a custom class called "Point":

Code 12.1 Overloading "+" operator

```
class Point:
    def __init__(self, x, y):
        self.x = x
        self.y = y
    def __add__(self, other):
        return Point(self.x + other.x, self.y + other.y)
p1 = Point(1, 2)
p2 = Point(3, 4)
p3 = p1 + p2
print(p3.x, p3.y)
```

In this example, the add method is used to add two Point objects together. The + operator is applied to two Point instances, p1 and p2, and the result is a third Point instance, p3, that represents the sum of the two.

12.2 Overloading '-' Operator in Python

To overload the "-" operator in Python, we can define the sub method in our custom class. The sub method takes two arguments, self and other, and is responsible for returning the result of subtracting the two objects.

Here's an example of how you might overload the "-" operator for a custom class called "Point":

Code 12.2 Overloading "-" operator in Python

```
class Point:
    def __init__(self, x, y):
        self.x = x
        self.y = y
    def __sub__(self, other):
        return Point(self.x - other.x, self.y - other.y)
```

```
p1 = Point(1, 2)
p2 = Point(3, 4)
p3 = p1 - p2
print(p3.x, p3.y)
```

In this example, the sub method is used to subtract two Point objects. The - operator is applied to two Point instances, p1 and p2, and the result is a third Point instance, p3, that represents the difference of the two.

12.3 Overloading Bitwise Operators

In Python, you can overload the bitwise operators such as &, |, ^, ~, <<, and >> by defining special methods in your class. The special methods for bitwise operations are __and__, __or__, __xor__, __invert__, __lshift__, and __rshift__, respectively.

Here's an example of how you might overload the bitwise operators for a custom class called "BitwiseOps":

Code 12.3 Overloading Bitwise operator in Python

```
class BitwiseOps:
    def __init__(self, value):
        self.value = value
    def __and__(self, other):
        return self.value & other.value
    def __or__(self, other):
        return self.value | other.value
    def __xor__(self, other):
        return self.value ^ other.value
    def __invert__(self):
        return ~self.value
    def __lshift__(self, shift):
        return self.value << shift
    def __rshift__(self, shift):
        return self.value >> shift
```

```
b1 = BitwiseOps(5)
b2 = BitwiseOps(3)
print(b1 & b2)
print(b1 | b2)
print(b1 ^ b2)
print(~b1)
print(b1 << 2)
print(b1 >> 1)
```

In this example, the BitwiseOps class overloads the bitwise operators. Instances of the BitwiseOps class are created and the bitwise operations are applied to those instances. The results of the operations are printed.

12.4 Overloading Relational Operators

In Python, you can overload relational operators such as '<', '>', '<=', '>=' and '==' using special methods called "lt", "gt", "le", "ge" and "eq" respectively.

These methods allow you to define custom comparison behavior for your classes, allowing you to compare objects based on specific attributes or conditions.

To overload a relational operator, you simply need to define the corresponding special method in your class and implement the desired comparison behavior.

Here's an example program that demonstrates how to overload the '<' operator in Python:

Code 12.4 Illustration of overloading '<' operator in Python

```
class Rectangle:
    def __init__(self, width, height):
        self.width = width
        self.height = height
    def area(self):
        return self.width * self.height
    def __lt__(self, other):
        return self.area() < other.area()
```

```
# Create two rectangles
rect1 = Rectangle(4, 5)
rect2 = Rectangle(3, 6)
# Compare the rectangles using the '<' operator
if rect1 < rect2:
    print("Rectangle 1 has a smaller area than Rectangle 2")
else:
    print("Rectangle 1 has a larger area than Rectangle 2")
```

In this program, we define a class Rectangle with attributes width and height, and methods area and __lt__. The area method calculates the area of the rectangle by multiplying the width and height. The __lt__ method overloads the ‘<’ operator and compares the areas of two rectangles.

We then create two instances of the Rectangle class and use the ‘<’ operator to compare them. The output of the program will depend on the dimensions of the rectangles we create. If rect1 has a smaller area than rect2, the program will print “Rectangle 1 has a smaller area than Rectangle 2”, otherwise it will print “Rectangle 1 has a larger area than Rectangle 2”.

12.5 Summary

In Python, we can customize the behavior of operators for our own classes by overloading them with special methods. We can overload various operators such as the addition and subtraction operators, bitwise operators, and relational operators. To overload the addition operator ‘+’, we use the special method “add”, and for the subtraction operator ‘-’, we use the “sub” method. For the bitwise operators ‘&’, ‘|’, ‘^’, and ‘~’, we can overload them with the “and”, “or”, “xor”, and “invert” methods respectively. We can also overload the relational operators such as ‘<’, ‘>’, ‘<=’, ‘>=’, and ‘==’ by defining the “lt”, “gt”, “le”, “ge”, and “eq” methods respectively. By overloading operators, we can define custom behavior for our classes that can simplify the code and make it more intuitive to use.

Review Questions

1. What is operator overloading in Python?
2. How can we overload the addition operator ‘+’ in Python?

3. What is the special method used to overload the subtraction operator '-' in Python?
4. How can we overload the bitwise operator '&' in Python?
5. What is the special method used to overload the relational operator '<' in Python?
6. Can we overload multiple operators in a single class in Python?
7. What is the benefit of overloading operators in Python?
8. How can we define custom behavior for our classes using operator overloading in Python?
9. What is the difference between the 'add' and 'radd' methods in Python?
10. Can we overload operators for built-in classes in Python?
11. Which special method is used to overload the addition operator '+' in Python?

    (a) add

    (b) sub

    (c) and

    (d) or
12. Which operator can we overload using the "eq" method in Python?

    (a) +

    (b) –

    (c) &

    (d) ==

Appendix-1
List of Python Standard Modules

Module Name	Description
array	Efficient arrays of numeric values
atexit	Register functions to be called when a program closes
audioop	Manipulate raw audio data
base64	Encode and decode binary data using Base64 representation
bdb	Debugger framework
binascii	Convert between binary and ASCII representations
bisect	Binary search and insertion into sorted lists
builtins	Built-in functions, exceptions, and attributes
cmath	Complex math functions
collections	Container datatypes
contextlib	Utilities for with-statement contexts
copy	Shallow and deep copy operations
csv	CSV file reading and writing
datetime	Basic date and time types
difflib	Helpers for computing deltas
dis	Disassembler for Python bytecode
email	Package for handling email messages
encodings	Encodings and Unicode handling
enum	Enumeration types
fileinput	Iterate over lines from multiple input sources
fnmatch	Unix-style filename pattern matching
fractions	Rational numbers
functools	Higher-order functions and operations on callable objects
gc	Garbage collector for Python
getpass	Portable password input

Module Name	Description
glob	Unix-style pathname pattern expansion
gzip	Support for gzip files
hashlib	Secure hash and message digest algorithms
heapq	Heap queue algorithm
html	Package for working with HTML
http	HTTP client and server
imaplib	IMAP email protocol client
imghdr	Determine the type of an image
importlib	Package for programmatically importing modules
inspect	Inspect live objects
io	Core tools for working with streams
ipaddress	IPv4/IPv6 manipulation library
itertools	Functions creating iterators for efficient looping
json	JSON encoder and decoder
logging	Flexible event logging system
lzma	Support for LZMA compression
math	Mathematical functions
mimetypes	Map filenames to MIME types
mmap	Memory-mapped file support
multiprocessing	Process-based parallelism
netrc	Read and write netrc files
nntplib	NNTP protocol client
numbers	Numeric abstract base classes
os	Miscellaneous operating system interfaces
pathlib	Object-oriented filesystem paths
pdb	Python debugger
pickle	Python object serialization
pkgutil	Package utilities
platform	Access to underlying platform's identifying data
plistlib	Generate and parse Mac OS X property lists
poplib	POP3 protocol client
pprint	Pretty-print data structures
profile	Performance analysis of Python programs
pstats	Statistics for Python programs

Module Name	Description
pty	Pseudo-terminal utilities
queue	Thread-safe FIFO implementation
quopri	Encode and decode MIME quoted-printable data
random	Generate pseudo-random numbers
re	Regular expression operations
reprlib	Alternate repr() implementation
resource	System resource usage information
RLcompleter	Completion function for GNU readline
runpy	Locate and run Python modules
sched	Event scheduler
secrets	Generate secure random numbers for managing secrets
select	Waiting for I/O completion
shelve	Python object persistence
shlex	Simple lexical analysis
shutil	High-level file operations
signal	Set handlers for asynchronous events
site	Site-specific configuration hook
smtpd	SMTP server classes
smtplib	SMTP protocol client
sndhdr	Determine the type of a sound file
socket	Low-level networking interface
socketserver	Framework for network servers
sqlite3	DB-API 2.0 interface for SQLite databases
ssl	TLS/SSL wrapper for socket objects
stat	Interpreting stat() results
statistics	Mathematical statistics functions
string	Common string operations
stringprep	Internet string preparation
struct	Interpret bytes as packed binary data
subprocess	Subprocess management
sunau	Read and write Sun AU files
symbol	Constants used with Python parse trees
symtable	Access to the compiler's symbol tables
sys	System-specific parameters and functions

Module Name	Description
sysconfig	Python's configuration information
tabnanny	Indentation validator
tarfile	Read and write tar archive files
telnetlib	Telnet client
tempfile	Generate temporary files and directories
textwrap	Text wrapping and filling
this	Prints the Zen of Python
threading	Thread-based parallelism
time	Time access and conversions
timeit	Measure execution time of small code snippets
tkinter	Python interface to Tcl/Tk
token	Constants used with Python parse trees
tokenize	Tokenize Python source code
trace	Trace or track Python statement execution
traceback	Print or retrieve a stack traceback
tracemalloc	Debug memory allocations
tty	Terminal control functions
turtle	Turtle graphics
turtledemo	A collection of Python turtle demos
types	Dynamic type creation and names for built-in types
typing	Support for type hints
unicodedata	Unicode database
unittest	Unit testing framework
urllib	URL handling modules
uu	Encode and decode uuencoded files
uuid	UUID objects according to RFC 4122
venv	Creation of virtual environments
warnings	Warning control
wave	Read and write WAV files
weakref	Weak references
webbrowser	Convenient web-browser controller
winreg	Windows registry access
winsound	Sound-playing interface for Windows
wsgiref	WSGI Utilities and Reference Implementation

Module Name	Description
xml	XML processing modules
xmlrpc	XMLRPC server and client modules
zipapp	Manage executable Python zip archives
zipfile	Manage executable Python zip archives
zipimport	Import modules from ZIP archives
zlib	Low-level interface to compression and decompression routines in the zlib library

Bibliography

1. Matthes, Eric. "Python Crash Course: A Hands-On, Project-Based Introduction to Programming." No Starch Press, 2019.
2. Ramalho, Luciano. "Fluent Python: Clear, Concise, and Effective Programming." O'Reilly Media, 2015.
3. Sweigart, Al. "Automate the Boring Stuff with Python: Practical Programming for Total Beginners." No Starch Press, 2015.
4. Lutz, Mark. "Learning Python: Powerful Object-Oriented Programming." O'Reilly Media, 2013.
5. VanderPlas, Jake. "Python Data Science Handbook: Essential Tools for Working with Data." O'Reilly Media, 2016.

Printed in the United States
by Baker & Taylor Publisher Services

Printed in the United States
by Baker & Taylor Publisher Services